LESSONS
FROM THE
HANOI
HILTON

LESSONS
FROM THE
HANOI
HILTON

SIX CHARACTERISTICS OF
HIGH-PERFORMANCE TEAMS

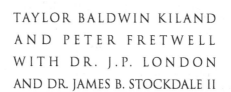

TAYLOR BALDWIN KILAND
AND PETER FRETWELL
WITH DR. J.P. LONDON
AND DR. JAMES B. STOCKDALE II

NAVAL INSTITUTE PRESS
ANNAPOLIS, MARYLAND

Naval Institute Press
291 Wood Road
Annapolis, MD 21402

The quotes by James Stockdale used in the side bars on pages 86 and 111
were reprinted from *Thoughts of a Philosophical Fighter Pilot,* by James B.
Stockdale, with the permission of the publisher, Hoover Institution Press.
Copyright ©1995 by the Board of Trustees of the Leland Stanford Junior
University.

All figures created by Matthew Simmons.

First Naval Institute Press paperback edition published in 2017.
ISBN: 978-1-68247-217-0 (paperback)

The Library of Congress has cataloged the hardcover edition as follows:
Fretwell, Peter.
  Lessons from the Hanoi Hilton : six characteristics of high performance
teams / Peter Fretwell and Taylor Baldwin Kiland ; with Dr. J. P. London.
    pages cm
  Includes bibliographical references and index.
  ISBN 978-1-61251-217-4 (hbk. : alk. paper) — ISBN 978-1-61251-
218-1 (ebook) 1. Vietnam War, 1961–1975—Prisoners and prisons,
North Vietnamese. 2. Prisoners of war—United States. 3. Prisoners of
war—Vietnam. 4. Leadership. 5. Resilience (Personality trait) I. Kiland,
Taylor Baldwin, date II. London, J. Phillip, date III. Title.
  DS559.4.F74 2013
  959.704'3—dc23

                                    2013001735

♾ This paper meets the requirements of ANSI/NISO z39.48-1992
(Permanence of Paper).

Printed in the United States of America.

25 24 23 22 21   13 12 11 10 9

Contents

List of Figures

About This Book

In this remarkable book Peter Fretwell and Taylor Kiland synthesize the collective experience and wisdom of men whose courage and loyalty is legendary. In younger years, I was honored to spend time surrounded by many of these men. Upon return from prison, they spoke of unity, strength, and a will to prevail in an atmosphere of brutality with an unconscious, clinical detachment that often stunned listeners. Their matter-of-fact delivery heightened the impact of their insights and quietly cut through the trivialities that seemed (then and now) so burdensome in modern life. Their humility was (and is) miraculous. Their continued loyalty to one another and dedication to their beliefs remain as durable as they are timeless.

Those of us who live with them have always sensed that the silent society they created—the invisible institutionalization of values, guidelines, and devotion to one another—might serve as a model for any family, group, or alliance that shares common purpose. Their struggle (in the end) might well inform a culture of mutual trust and commitment essential to productivity and healthy communities. Many authors have tried to articulate the lessons that might lead to such a model—but (with all due respect) the attempts I have read are either 'too close' to the experience or struggle to comprehend its breadth and depth. To be fair, this difficulty is very understandable as the subject matter consists of what classical scholars denote as "universals."

Peter Fretwell and Taylor Kiland have interviewed, studied, and examined the narratives and issues of these men with deliberate focus for the last seven years. Their gift to us in this remarkably well-written compendium is the distillation of life lessons for those seeking practical application. They clearly set forth "what we can learn" from those who created their own civilization. As the authors have winnowed through thousands of pages and sources, they have centered relentlessly on the traits, behaviors, and practices that lead to shaping a *high performing team*.

In *Lessons from the Hanoi Hilton*, the authors render a ready guide for the formation and nurturing of teams that perform with fluid motion and what appears to be effortless communication. They elaborate and build on exemplars dedicated to loyalty, honesty, clarity of mission, and values that sustain unity. The authors have, in essence, created a curriculum for study and implementation of these practical concepts that are vital to any organization.

I have long found it ironic that the cynical name "Hanoi Hilton" clings to the experience of the brave souls who shed their blood within its high, thick double walls. Built by the French and designed to de-humanize its inhabitants with shards of broken champagne bottles serving as provincial razor wire, it stood in the middle of Hanoi. Several North Vietnamese political leaders at the time of the American war had spent time in its cells and leg-irons during the fifties. The complex was a labyrinth constructed to disorient inmates and its actual name was Hoa Lo—'Fiery Furnace.'

The 'Furnace,' (even with its horrors) might serve as metaphor in retrospect. The isolated, compressed experience of those who survived there was, I submit, a refiner's fire—a deep foundry in which precious metals are brought to searing temperatures over and again until they reach their most pure (and precious) state. So it was with the men of Hoa Lo walking away united and phenomenally refined—a gold standard of our country—precious metal in a world with much too much slag and dross. In many ways, this gem of a book accompanies their excellence—an excellence as difficult as it is rare.

Finally, this work praises my father and (in many ways) anoints him as a leader of men. He has been praised in many ways. But the reader should know that during thoughtful days in quiet moments Dad would share his soul with me and others—pouring out his incredible admiration and respect for each man with whom he served during difficult days.

While I hesitate to speak for him, the man I knew and loved would want to allocate any acclaim, fully share any tribute, and thoroughly distribute any glory associated with his contributions. Without the strength and courage of each and every man, his thoughts and words would have been an empty vessel. Dad knew, in the end, that leadership is nothing if not for the willingness of those who follow. He stands *among* his men—men who returned with honor.

James Bond Stockdale II, PhD

Foreword

The prisoner of war (POW) experience is unimaginable to most of us. Even more unimaginable is the idea that something positive could come of it. For the Vietnam POWs of the Hanoi Hilton, the possibility of survival rested on finding something positive and developing a culture around it. That positive goal was Return with Honor, and an entire culture was created to unify and motivate the POWs not only to survive the harrowing experience, but to come home with dignity.

It may also surprise some people that many facets of the POW culture are shared by successful individuals and organizations. It's true that as part of the U.S. military, the POWs already belonged to a successful organization with a strong culture. However, as *Lessons from the Hanoi Hilton* reveals, there were specific values and actions adopted to overcome the Vietnam prisoner of war experience that transcended the military experience.

As a 1959 graduate of the U.S. Naval Academy and a former Navy pilot, I have a very similar background to many of the Hanoi POWs—*before* their experience. The most important lessons that I have learned in life have been applicable not only to my military career, but also to my civilian career in government contracting and my personal life.

All military pilots back in my day had to participate in a training exercise called the Dilbert Dunker drill. The drill simulated an airplane crashing into the water by dropping a mock airplane cockpit down a twenty-five-foot ramp into a large, deep pool. I was trained to brace for the impact, free myself from shoulder and seat harnesses, and swim to the surface. The point of the exercise wasn't just learning to escape from a submerged airplane. It was to see if Navy pilots could also handle a mild crisis and a touch of trauma. As a pilot, waiting for the cage to drop, looked down the ramp, all sorts of nerves emerged and doubts raced through his head. The key to success was learning to control your emotions and let your training take over. Along with countless others, I successfully completed the drill, but the lesson that has always stayed with me is this: No matter what the situation is, you can control your response to it.

This lesson was at the center of the POW culture, as Kiland and Fretwell explain so well in this book. The prisoners could not control their environment or their treatment. They could, however, control how they reacted to each experience. They found ways to communicate to one another and establish common responses (with acceptable variations) to each challenge. I'm sure this lesson transcends many facets of all our lives.

As Kiland and Fretwell mapped the lessons they learned from the Hanoi POWs, I could also clearly see how they applied not only to me but also to my organization. For twenty-three years I was CEO of CACI International, an information technology and professional services company, and I still serve as executive chairman and chairman of the board. I also had to create a culture that unified and motivated everyone to achieve common goals. Of course, the resources I had were considerable compared with those of the Hanoi POWs, but the fundamentals are very much the same.

Just as the POW culture was captured with "Return with Honor," CACI's culture is represented by our motto "Ever Vigilant." While mottos are important, they need to be put into action. I have found that the one thing that all high-performing and sustainable organizations share is orientation on a mission. Establishing a mission creates a common purpose, defines priorities, and helps decide how to allocate resources. It also puts into perspective what is and is not important. For the Hanoi POWs, the mission everyone focused on was getting each prisoner home without anyone feeling shame or disappointment for what they endured or had to do to survive. For example, Kiland and Fretwell refer to two POWs who overcame racial differences to help each other through their ordeal. What would have kept the two men apart back in the United States was no longer relevant in Hanoi.

It is essential that any organization similarly establish its core values, clearly articulate expectations, and learn from its experiences. Some people may discount the importance of a strong organizational culture or reduce it to a collection of documents. In response, I point to Enron, WorldCom, Lehman Brothers, Countrywide, and many other companies that are no longer with us because they either ignored the principles of a viable organizational culture or only gave lip service to them. CACI has worked hard on developing and sharing its culture— and we recently celebrated our fiftieth year in business in 2012. An astonishing number of Hanoi POWs returned home after the war—with honor and little or no adverse effects. Hardly a coincidence, I'd say.

Over the years I have had the honor of meeting many Hanoi Hilton POWs. I even have the privilege to call a few of them my friends. In 2003 CACI hosted a reception for *Open Doors: Vietnam POWs Thirty Years Later*, an exhibit and book by Taylor Kiland and Jamie Howren. This exhibit of thirty photographs and narratives profiles some of the Vietnam era's longest held prisoners of war, who overcame the terrible ordeal of captivity to return to America and build successful careers. CACI later acquired the collection, and it is on display at CACI headquarters. I pass these profiles every day. Whether it is the men I personally know or those I know by reputation, I have the same thought as I look at their pictures: May we all be as resilient and resolute as they were in service to our country and in life. As true role models, that may be the greatest honor we can give them.

Dr. J. P. London
Captain, USNR (Ret.)
Chairman of the Board
CACI International Inc

Preface:
The Man in the Corner Cell

On what he called a "milk run" on September 9, 1965, James Bond Stockdale was flying his A-4 Skyhawk toward the Thanh Hoa Bridge, just south of Hanoi. Destroying this bridge was proving to be a tough mission; the air wing based on board the USS *Oriskany* had been "bouncing" 500-pound bombs for several weeks.

On this particular day the attack force was going to try something different. Stockdale was leading thirty-five planes carrying a "special" load: 2,000-pounders. The mission took some creative engineering, including jury-rigging some switches to hang the bombs off the wings, pumping out some of the fuel to maintain takeoff weight limits, and then conducting an in-flight refueling en route to the target. The bridge was a key objective, as it was becoming a symbol of resistance for the North Vietnamese. Unfortunately, the weather that day was not cooperating. The ceiling and visibility were zero-zero. So the planes diverted to a secondary target: a series of boxcars on a railroad siding between Vinh and Thanh Hoa. These targets required descending below ten thousand feet.

Supremely confident, at the top of his game and the pinnacle of his career, Stockdale described his almost cavalier attitude that day: "As I glided toward that easy target, I felt totally self-satisfied. I had the top combat job that a Navy commander can hold, and I was in tune with my environment. I was comfortable with the people I worked with, and I knew the trade so well that I often improvised variations in accepted procedures and encouraged others to do so under my watchful eye."[1]

Suddenly he heard the "boom-boom-boom" of a 57-mm antiaircraft gun from just behind his wingtip, and in seconds his plane was inoperable. Stockdale recalled, "I was hit—all

the red lights came on, my control system was going out—
and I could barely keep that plane from flying into the ground
while I got the oxygen mask to my mouth so I could tell my
wingman that I was about to eject." Eject, eject, eject! In an
instant, Stockdale left the world he knew.

Slowly floating down to earth in his parachute, Stockdale
had moments to reflect, and he saw, not flashbacks, but a
flashfuture: "When I ejected from that plane in 1965, I left
the world of technology and entered the world of Epictetus."[2]

Epictetus? The Stoic? Why? To understand Stockdale's
thought process requires an understanding of his educational
background. Stockdale had delved into philosophy for the first
time when he was completing a master's degree in political science at Stanford. A philosophy professor and World War II
Navy veteran, Dr. Philip Rhinelander, introduced him to the
ancient Greeks and became a mentor. The two were clearly
simpatico. Stockdale found a strong personal belief system in
the words of the Stoics. He was fascinated by the discussion of
the quality of human nature when the human is stripped bare.
But he wasn't sure whether the philosophical approach had
applications in a military environment until the last time he
and Dr. Rhinelander met. He recalled, "At our last private session, Dr. Rhinelander noted that I was a military man; for that
reason he gave me a copy of *The Enchiridion* by Epictetus, the
son of a Roman slave. This writing was what might be considered a manual for the combat officer of his time."[3]

The Enchiridion preached personal responsibility and a
"choose your battle" approach to life. Its first edict begins, "Of
things some are in our power, and others are not. . . . And the
things in our power are by nature free, not subject to restraint
nor hindrance: but the things not in our power are weak, slav-
ish, subject to restraint, in the control of others."[4] The opera-
tive word is "free."

ENTERING THE WORLD OF EPICTETUS

As Stockdale floated slowly down to certain capture and imprisonment by the North Vietnamese enemy, he recalled the wisdom of Epictetus: "I remembered the basic truth of *subjective consciousness* as *the ability to distinguish what is in my power from that which is not*. I recalled that 'lameness is an impediment to the leg, but not to the will,' and I knew that *self-discipline* would provide the balance I would need in this contest of high stakes [italics added]."[5]

Understanding the link between Epictetus, Stockdale's towering intellect, and the eventual success of the prisoner of war (POW) culture is critical. Researchers who have studied the POWs extensively say that Stockdale's philosophical essays can be obtuse and dauntingly hard for most people to understand.[6] It is possible to read all Stockdale's writings about the Hanoi Hilton and still not clearly see the connection between Epictetus and how the POWs' high-performance culture evolved. But the link exists, and understanding it is the key to replicating it.

When he arrived at the Hanoi Hilton, Stockdale entered a world in which many POWs had already shown selflessness and commitment to each other. But some officers took the attitude sometimes seen in POW camps in Korea and other wars: the fast and agile survived; the slow and injured were sacrificed. As one of the senior ranking officers (SROs), Stockdale chose to accept the mantle of leadership, both the risks and opportunities of being in charge. Stockdale relied on the philosophy he had adopted and internalized some four years prior while studying at Stanford.

He knew he should follow the military's Code of Conduct for POWs, the rules that govern conduct of American prisoners of war. The code, established in 1955, reaffirms that under the Geneva Conventions, POWs should give only "name, rank, service number, and date of birth" and requires that under interrogation, captured military personnel should "evade answering further questions to the utmost of my ability." Stockdale knew these guidelines wouldn't be enough.

And so he dug into his bag of memories from his studies, looking for useful tools. He recalled the Epictetus edicts as outlined in *The Enchiridion*: "men are disturbed not by things, but by the view they take of them"; "do not be concerned with things which are beyond your power"; and "demand not that events should happen as you wish, but wish them to happen as they do happen and you will go on well."[7] In other words, you get to choose how you view your current plight. You get to choose how you react to it.

Soon after arriving at the Hoa Lo Prison in Hanoi, Stockdale's worst fears were realized. A young naval officer in the cell across the hall from him, Rod Knutson, was refusing to answer any questions not covered by the Code of Conduct and was being threatened with death for his resistance. Knutson knew he was within earshot of other POWs and shouted out what was happening to him. Over the next six days he was brutally beaten, whipped, bound, and kept in leg stocks. But he wouldn't budge.

So the North Vietnamese introduced a particularly nasty torture called the "rope trick." The captor would tie Knutson's wrists together behind his back until circulation was cut off and then bend him forward, causing excruciating pain and claustrophobia. It was an insidious but brilliant move on the part of the North Vietnamese. There was little chance the rope trick would cause death, but it took most men to their breaking point and produced results. They talked. Stockdale realized that the dynamic had shifted: "Henceforth, Americans were to be allowed to stay within the bounds of name, rank, serial number, and date of birth only *at North Vietnam's sufferance* [italics added]."[8]

STOCKDALE'S INNOVATION

Stockdale and his fellow POWs faced a Hobson's choice. They learned quickly that they would all eventually break under enough torture and thus violate the Code of Conduct and risk military disgrace. If they resisted, they would continue to be tortured until they submitted—for information that had no intelligence value and that was certainly not worth their life or a limb.

Indeed, when Stockdale was asked to write a letter to the U.S. government denouncing the war effort, he initially refused. Subjected to the rope trick, he eventually submitted and gave his captors a statement. Stockdale soon realized that he had to expand the Code of Conduct in order to give the POWs some flexibility and the fledgling POW organization a chance to survive. The POWs were at risk of falling into the familiar pattern of "every man for himself" so often seen in prisons and other life-and-death environments.

Stockdale made a difficult decision that laid the foundation for a self-sustaining organization. He instructed the POWs to resist their captors to the best of their ability, but not at the cost of permanent harm. If they reached their breaking point, they should fall back on deceit and distortion—giving false, misleading, or ludicrous information. Finally, Stockdale insisted that the POWs force their captors to start over at each interrogation session. This innovation allowed for failure in the moment without failure in the mission.

These strategies and tactics conformed to the Code of Conduct where they could. When necessary, Stockdale created a new path by giving each POW the responsibility of deciding how to resist. Collectively, under these new guidelines, the POWs set a goal of giving every man a chance to achieve their group mission: Return with Honor.

This act earned the POWs' respect. Stockdale, after all, shared their pain (literally) and understood the seemingly impossible predicament these men faced. Effective resistance couldn't be centered on Herculean displays of pain tolerance or arbitrary goal lines. Instead, Stockdale made commitment, persistence, and unity (or a unified response) the driving objectives. Stockdale was, by virtue of his rank, the man in the corner cell—the boss. But decisions like this made him their leader.

Chronology of
a High-Performance Culture

AUGUST 5, 1964

Everett Alvarez, Jr. becomes the first American military aviator shot down and taken captive in North Vietnam. A week
after his capture he is trucked to Hanoi and placed in an old
French prison, Hoa Lo, later dubbed the "Hanoi Hilton" by its
occupants. He spent eight years and seven months as a POW,
making him the second-longest-held POW in American military history.

MARCH 1965

Operation Rolling Thunder begins. Navy and Air Force pilots
launch more than fifteen hundred sorties a month against
North Vietnam, and pilots start joining Alvarez in the Hanoi
Hilton.

JUNE 1965

One of the POWs, Carlyle "Smitty" Harris, recalls a tap code
that an instructor had shown him during a coffee break at Air
Force survival school. The most powerful tool for spreading
the POW culture is born.

SEPTEMBER 9, 1965

James Stockdale is shot down and becomes a POW. Stockdale—
along with Robinson "Robbie" Risner and Jeremiah Denton
Jr.—steps up and serve as the senior ranking officers for much
of the next seven years.

1967–69

The period called "the middle years" brings the highest number
of POW fatalities and injuries, largely attributable to harsher
living conditions and more intense brutality. Conditions before
1967 had been less severe, and conditions later in the war will

be more tolerable as the North Vietnamese face international scrutiny for their treatment of the POWs.

APRIL 1967

More than 170 American pilots are housed in the Hanoi Hilton.

OCTOBER 1967

Eleven of the camp's "troublemakers" (the term used by the North Vietnamese; Stockdale called his ten compatriots his "heroes") are moved to the Ministry of National Defense in Hanoi in a futile attempt to isolate them and squelch resistance. They dub their new home "Alcatraz." (Groups of POWs were moved into and out of fifteen different locations between 1965 and 1973 for reasons ranging from political propaganda to fear of rescue attempts.)

NOVEMBER 1970

U.S. commandos attempt to rescue about fifty POWs held at the Son Tay prison camp in an action known as the Son Tay raid. The POWs had been moved, but the bold rescue effort scares the North Vietnamese into moving all prisoners to the Hanoi Hilton in order to consolidate security against another rescue attempt.

CHRISTMAS 1970

"Camp Unity" becomes the prison moniker as most POWs in North Vietnam are consolidated in the Hanoi Hilton. By the end of 1970 Camp Unity houses more than 340 U.S. POWs.

1971–73

As air strikes increase over North Vietnam, groups of POWs are moved to other locations throughout North Vietnam.

FEBRUARY 1971

The so-called church riot establishes the solidarity of the POWs in Camp Unity. While the later years of captivity are generally less brutal, uncertainty about when the prisoners will be released and fears about whether their careers are being derailed at home bring new challenges for maintaining the mission focus.

MAY 1972

More than two hundred POWs are moved to "Dogpatch," a camp less than ten miles from the Chinese border with North Vietnam.

JANUARY 27, 1973

The last POW captured over North Vietnam, Phillip Kientzler, is shot down, and the Paris Peace Accords are signed.

FEBRUARY 12, 1973

The first Americans repatriated by Operation Homecoming arrive at Clark Air Base in the Philippines. Denton speaks for the group, stepping before the microphones and cameras to say, "We are honored to have had the opportunity to serve our country under difficult circumstances."

LESSONS
FROM THE
HANOI
HILTON

Introduction

In the modern era of high turnover rates and short company tenures, clearly defined and pervasive corporate cultures based on strongly held values are becoming increasingly rare. Yet a strong and sustainable culture allows for significant differentiation and can be used as a competitive weapon in a dynamic and difficult global marketplace. This book will show how a group of men, thrust into extremely difficult and trying circumstances in a faraway prison in North Vietnam, built a high-performing, resilient organizational culture—one that persists to this day.

Thrust into a crucible unlike anything in history, these POWs formed a high-performance team that reached its goal of returning home with honor and with reputations intact. Held between 1964 and 1973 at the infamous Hanoi Hilton— the nickname for Hoa Lo, a former French prison where the vast majority of the aviators shot down and captured in North Vietnam were held prisoner—they remained unified in their resistance to the enemy and in their loyalty to their country for nearly nine years in captivity. Even more remarkably, they have managed to keep alive the sense of purpose and meaning they created from their experience. The lessons gleaned from their time in North Vietnam are aiding later generations of military men and women, as well as businesses, governments, and communities. Their legacy and success will outlive them.

DR. SLEDGE'S EPIPHANY

Dr. William Sledge would walk outside his office just before his next appointment to watch his patients walk down the hall. He wanted to size them up from afar before he interviewed them up close. He could always pick out the fighter jet jocks. They had a certain bearing—a swagger, really—that was distinctive. Their uniforms were never exactly perfect—almost intentionally so. They often arrived late for their appointments with him. The bomber pilots, in contrast, were always precisely on time, and their uniforms were perfectly regulation. Sledge was an Air Force psychiatrist tasked with evaluating the pilots' mental health. In most cases, he was younger than his patients. Was he intimidated? "I was too unaware to be intimidated," he recalled—unaware of the extent of the ordeal the men he was about to see had endured for years.[1]

It had been more than a year since the POWs from the Vietnam War had been released from captivity in the Hanoi Hilton. Now, the war was almost over. But these men were still serving on active duty in the Air Force, and some were trying to return to the cockpit after a long absence and a traumatic experience. So the Air Force wanted to evaluate them closely for fitness—physical and mental. Sledge was one of the doctors assigned to conduct the evaluations.

He had been told they were a "mixed bag"—some damaged by the experience, some faring much better. He had access to the classified debriefings the men had received immediately upon their release and was stunned by their first-person accounts of the brutality of their incarceration. Thus, he was not sure what to expect as they arrived for their individual evaluations with him. Watching them walk down the hall to their appointments, he immediately noticed less of a swagger and maybe a bit more grace. They seemed more humble and grateful to him. An outsider probably wouldn't have noticed the subtle difference, but Sledge did.

One by one, he asked them questions about how they were adjusting to freedom, to being back on active duty, and to reunification with their families. From their responses, an unusual pattern emerged. Most of them revealed a series of tangible and intangible benefits from their POW experience: improved personal relationships and altered values with regard to their careers, for example. They also talked extensively about the close bonds they had formed in prison. Several said they had never had such intense relationships as they had with their roommates and fellow prisoners in the Hanoi Hilton. One patient seemed almost "wistful" to Sledge when he admitted that he missed prison. After sixty to eighty of these interviews, during which Sledge heard some of the same sentiments over and over again, the doctor knew he had stumbled upon a phenomenon. The men described their lives as improved as a result of their POW experience. Sledge decided to explore this theory and see if statistics validated it. He convinced the Air Force to pay for a more comprehensive study of the POWs. And in the fall of 1976 he teamed up with two of his colleagues in the Air Force, Col. James A. Boydstun and Alton J. Rabe, to develop a questionnaire that was mailed to all repatriated Air Force POWs still on active duty. The POWs were divided into two subgroups—those who were captured before October 1969 and those who were captured after December 1971.[2] Bombing of North Vietnam had ceased from October 1969 to December 1971, and no POWs were shot down or captured during the break. Those captured in 1969 or earlier were held in captivity a minimum of forty months, whereas those captured after the break were held a maximum of sixteen months. The "early shoot-downs" thus experienced a much longer period of captivity and more mistreatment. The researchers wanted to know whether there were any significant differences between these two groups of POWs.

LOOKING FOR ANSWERS

The questionnaire was also sent to a matched control group. The control group was a comparable population that consisted of pilots and navigators demographically similar to the POWs. They were of similar age, military rank, and military expertise, and they had deployed to Southeast Asia on a combat tour at least once. A total of 221 POWs and 341 control subjects voluntarily responded to the questionnaire.

The researchers had developed a fourteen-question survey that was based on studies of POWs from the Korean War and literature available on both the World War II and Korean War POWs. The topics addressed ranged from marital status and current educational pursuits to the presence of injuries, a ranking of problems after repatriation, the degree of suffering during and after captivity, and whether or not significant mental changes had occurred as a result of the captivity experience.

The results supported Sledge's hypothesis: the POWs from both periods of the war reported more benefits from their wartime experience than the control group did. Sixty-one percent of the POWs who answered the questionnaire indicated "favorable significant mental changes," while only 32 percent of the control group felt the same benefits.[3] The examples cited in clinical evaluations of these changes included more self-awareness, increased optimism, a reprioritization of the relative importance of family and career, and renewed political or religious values. The POW experience seemed to bring these men more clarity and perspective in their lives. Even more interesting, the Vietnam POWs reported more subjective benefits of their POW experience than those POWs from the Korean War: 61 percent of Vietnam respondents perceived benefits, whereas only 21 percent of the Korean War respondents did.[4]

Sledge's study was published in the *Archives of General Psychiatry* in 1980, seven years after the POWs had returned home and long before the term "resiliency" was coined and used in reference to combat veterans. It was the first study to identify the surprisingly positive outcome that pervaded this group of men, the longest-held group of POWs in our nation's history and one that remained unified and strong throughout years of torturous captivity. What it didn't address is why the men fared so well. What about these men made them particularly resilient to the long-term effects of posttraumatic stress disorder (PTSD)? What about this POW experience made more of the Vietnam War POWs—as compared with their Korean War POW counterparts—report that, on balance, they benefited from their captivity experience? Why were they so successful as a group and as individuals?

FROM THE 30,000-FOOT LEVEL: THREE ELEMENTS OF A SUSTAINABLE CULTURE

From the highest level view, the POW culture developed at the Hanoi Hilton can be defined by three concepts: virtual leadership, viral culture, and a social network. These elements were provided by James Stockdale. He was one of the senior ranking officers (SROs) in the Hanoi Hilton. He wasn't the only SRO to lead the POWs, but he was one of the most influential.

1. **Virtual leadership.** Stockdale established and cemented his leadership role "virtually"; that is, he defined the mission, credo, and rules of the road—or daily practices—for the organization without a physical presence. He laid the foundation for the cultural norms that were developed and perpetuated. And he helped the individuals in this organization stay committed to and inspired by the mission through his own personal behavior—behavior he modeled for everyone else.

Stockdale risked his life for his fellow POWs in several incidents; one such incident earned him the Medal of Honor. But, even if he had lost his life in captivity, the mission and the organization were so strong, so powerful, so unified, and so personally meaningful that they would have survived—indeed, thrived—in his absence.

2. **Viral culture.** A viral culture spreads the goals and guidelines of the organization willingly and fluidly. When individual followers embrace and own the group mission—because they know their interests are protected—and when their mission involves commonly held values, cultural norms

spread. Instead of competing with each other for morsels, the individual POWs collaborated with each other to reach their high-performance goal. When their own best interests were intertwined with the group's mission, the positive peer pressure to finish the job went "viral" in the organization.

3. Social network. The social network perpetuated and nurtured the culture with inclusive communication and the expectation that each person would do what they could to help the mission and others in the group. The POWs' social network grew from a mixture of support and competition, nurture and challenge, individuality and collaboration.

FROM THE GROUND LEVEL: SIX CHARACTERISTICS OF SUSTAINABLE, HIGH-PERFORMANCE CULTURES

A close examination of how Stockdale and the POWs built their culture shows that these three broad elements offered a simple but strong framework for creating an organization with staying power. Over time the POW group also developed six specific characteristics that any organization can replicate:

1. **The Mission Leads.** A sustainable, high-performance culture is mission-centric, not leader-centric. Leaders and followers may change, but the mission of a sustainable culture does not change.

2. **You Are Your Brother's Keeper.** A sustainable, high-performance culture's leaders protect followers by creating an environment of inclusion, honesty, and second chances. Leaders and followers are responsible for caring for the needs of others while still challenging them to grow and learn.

3. **Think Big and Basically.** The rules of the road in a sustainable, high-performance culture are minimal, simple, and focused on achieving the mission. Individuals and

small teams are entrusted with personal responsibility and authority in most daily decisions.

4. **Don't Piss Off the Turnkey.** A sustainable, high-performance culture stresses effectiveness (determining what works best in pursuit of the mission) and efficiency (strictly reserving resources and energies for what can be controlled) in pursuit of its mission.

5. **Keeping the Faith.** A sustainable, high-performance culture is dominated by rational beliefs and optimism. Its members are willing to face their fears and take risks. They view setbacks and failures as temporary, local, and external—not permanent, pervasive, or personal. They use failure as a learning mechanism—part of the high price of success—in their relentless pursuit of the mission.

6. **The Power of We.** A sustainable, high-performance culture finds personal and organizational meaning in what its members are trying to achieve (why the mission matters) and in the commonly embraced values that connect followers to the mission (how they are connected).

Leaders who want to create a sustainable, high-performance culture in their organization—one that is strong enough to outlast changes in leaders and followers—must nurture these six characteristics. The POWs held in the Hanoi Hilton are a case study in how it can be done.

CHAPTER 1

The Rosetta Stone: Performance Enhancement

No one comes to a fall by another man's deed.

—EPICTETUS

On a raw November day in the Hudson Valley, cadets walked between classes at the U.S. Military Academy's Center for Enhanced Performance (CEP). They braced themselves against the weather as they passed the wall of windows at one end of a conference room. The view from the conference room window offered a broad swath of U.S. military history. West Point, the oldest military academy in the country and the training ground for both the heroic and silent warriors our nation has produced, is home to the CEP, a modern research center in the midst of more than two centuries of tradition.

From the front of the conference room, Dr. Nathaniel Zinsser, director of the Performance Enhancement Program at CEP, launched into what seemed to be a standard speech about the origins of the sports psychology–based program at West Point: "We work to enhance human performance. We study the underlying psychological and mental skills that are characteristic of Super Bowl champions, and the . . . Michael Jordans of the world."[1]

The sports psychology model was more than just a good fit for the CEP—it was Zinsser's only choice when he decided to study enhancing human performance in challenging situations. He said, "When this program started in 1989, the only field of study that looked at those intangibles of human performance and treated them as learnable skills was this emerging field of applied sports psychology."[2] Could high-performance sports training be relevant to the Vietnam POW experience? Could it help explain how these men created such a strong and resilient organization?

Zinsser put the theory of sports psychology into perspective and gave it some gravitas by linking it with the most unlikely of partners—ancient philosophy: "Applied sports psychology has deep roots that tap into the training of warriors from various cultures. We see the same methodology expressed in the training of young men and women for war—going back to the *Bhagavad-Gita*, where Krishna incarnates as the charioteer for the young warrior, Arjuna, and says, 'You've got to get out of your self-limitations, see the field, and understand what you can and can't do as a human being.'" Using sports metaphors, Zinsser recited the basic tactics the POWs used to survive and thrive in an environment designed to crush their spirits: "You control what you can and refuse to invest energy in what you can't control. That is a fundamental piece of any quality training in applied sports psychology. You can't control how the pitcher throws the ball to you. You can't control the weather. You can't control the call of the referee. You can't control the fact that your receiver dropped a perfect pass in a crucial situation. How good are you at letting go of all that and then returning to what you can control?"[3]

He continued, "You don't look to anyone or anything besides your desired outcome, and you use that as a benchmark or a framework for all the momentary decisions that you have to make day by day, hour by hour, minute by minute—to ensure that those decisions move you toward your desired outcome."[4]

In a few minutes' time Zinsser connected the dots between three seemingly disparate subjects—ancient philosophers, elite athletes and performance enhancement, and the world of the POWs—by articulating the unifying piece that brings research, theories, and personal stories into focus. He provided the how, whereas most of the research sought to explain why these methods worked.

~ The Tap Code: The POWs' Social Network ~

In the spring of 1967 Orson Swindle was in his fifth month as a POW and suffering in solitary confinement. His cellblock consisted of about eight cells with thick walls and no way to see other POWs in the camp. Sometimes his fellow prisoners could whisper under the door, but most of their communications were achieved through a knuckle-tapping system they called the "tap code." The code was introduced by Carlyle "Smitty" Harris, who had learned it while at military survival school. It consisted of a five-by-five matrix of the alphabet (K was deleted from the matrix, and C was used for both C and K). A letter was identified by its location on the matrix. The first number identified the letter's row location and the second number identified the letter's column location. So, "S" would be 4-3, four taps followed by three taps.

Swindle remembers a POW being moved into a cell about three cells down from him. Being without a roommate, Swindle was eager to talk.

The next day, when the guards vacated the block, I was down on the floor whispering to the "new guy," to identify himself and join in the communications stream. Commander James Bond Stockdale checked in. I was overwhelmed by his presence. Here next to me was our leader, a prisoner since 1965 and the senior Navy captive, and I was in direct contact with him. We were faintly aware of his most recent ordeal. Our admiration for him is difficult to describe. In the days that followed, Jim was not communicating much, as he was recovering both physically and mentally from pain recently inflicted. Sadly, there was to be much more suffering for him.

One day we young officers were discussing some issue and not finding answers. I whispered down the passageway, "Hang on for a minute, and let me ask the Old Man what we should do." Commander Stockdale came up after a couple of calls, and responded with a wise answer to our problem.

(continued)

Now fast forward to early February, 1973, almost six years later. We have been told we are going home. In the large courtyard area of Hoa Lo prison (the Hanoi Hilton), the North Vietnamese are allowing one large cell of Americans at a time to wander over to the recently uncovered windows of other cells that surrounded the courtyard, permitting conversation. I see a slight man, terribly worn and tired looking with very gray hair limping over to my window. He looks up at me, smiles and says, "Hi, I'm Jim Stockdale, who are you?" We literally had never seen each other.

I reply, "Sir, I am Orson Swindle, and I want to thank you for all the leadership and the inspiration you have provided to me, to all of us. Your leadership and personal conduct helped me survive this past six years. You very likely saved my life." I continue, "I remember a day back in the spring of 1967, when you moved in to my area of the cellblock. My morale and self-esteem were pretty low then. I was really down on myself. I recall how having you around and knowing what you had endured reminded me of my duty, my obligations, and what was expected of me. You inspired me by your presence. I am eternally indebted to you."

Jim smiles and says, "Orson, I remember you and those difficult days so well. I was really depressed and down on myself, too. I want you to know that when you whispered, "Hang on for a minute, and let me ask the Old Man what we should do," you reminded me of who I was and of my duty to each of you. Orson, you helped me survive, too."[1]

Even though they had not met each other face-to-face, Stockdale and Swindle had made a social connection, and an indelible bond had been formed. Stockdale had effectively reasserted his leadership position, and the POWs had been reassured of his commitment.

Stockdale's most basic command to new pilots entering the camp was "Get on the wall!" Learn the tap code and share information. Help each other. Support each other. Remind each other of the mission and each POW's role in that mission. Information was passed from cell to adjacent cell. When one person or cell dropped out, the communications network broke down. Everyone had to be included, or there was no network. From cell to cell, the POWs created their own social network. Information was power, and it was shared with everyone.

---

[1] Orson Swindle, "Always Leading and Always Will," *Proceedings*, August 2005, 64.

AN UNCOMMON BOND

The link between these different worlds was long ago recognized by some of the POWs themselves. Long before Lance Armstrong became a household name, Chuck Boyd befriended him, thanks to their shared experience with cancer and their love of cycling. Boyd, a former Vietnam POW and retired Air Force four-star general, lost his first wife to cancer and survived his own bout with the disease. Lance Armstrong was a professional bicycle racer who survived cancer. Even after Armstrong became a controversial and tarnished figure, their friendship endured because Chuck Boyd learned long ago to value friends regardless of a fickle public's acclaim or outcry of the moment.

They first met in 1993, when Boyd was deputy commander in chief, U.S. European Command. He was invited as a guest of the Tour de France, and he accompanied Armstrong's sponsor, Motorola, on the tour.

Armstrong was less than half Boyd's age and had never served in the military. Boyd's best biking trips were long rides on one of his Ducati or BMW motorcycles. They seemingly had little in common. But they kept in touch. As Boyd described the relationship, "We had a rapport." When Armstrong was diagnosed with cancer, Boyd was one of the few who learned the news before the public did. Armstrong called him thirty minutes before he made his announcement.

Several years later, after he beat his cancer into remission, Armstrong decided to try to win the 1999 Tour de France. Boyd thought, "Good luck with that!" But the general kept his doubts to himself and promised Armstrong, "Lance, if you are in the lead as you head into Paris, I will be there to greet you on the finish line."

Months later Boyd was on a motorcycle trip in northern Maine, enjoying a few weeks of vacation. One Wednesday morning in July, he happened to pick up a local paper and read the sports section, something he rarely did. The headline reported that Armstrong was leading the Tour de France and was expected to ride to victory on Sunday.

Surprised, Boyd chuckled to himself, knowing what he had to do—and he had less than three days to do it. He called his secretary and told her to book him on a Washington to Paris flight on Friday. He packed a small bag, revved up his motorcycle, and headed south on Thursday morning. Thirteen hours and twenty-five minutes later, he wearily arrived back home in Washington, packed fresh clothing, and jumped on his plane to Paris. As promised, "I was standing at the finish line in Paris cheering for Lance. Every year for seven years I was on that finish line. The deal was, 'You're leading coming into Paris, I'll be on the finish line.'"[5]

A CULTURE OF HYPERFOCUSED, NO EXCUSES, "ALL-IN" COMMITMENT

Boyd agrees that sports psychology techniques mirror those used by the Hanoi Hilton POWs in facing their adversaries. And he still believes Armstrong has demonstrated the same focus that the POWs employed. As Boyd told Armstrong, "Lance, you would've made a helluva POW!"[6]

Before he was stripped of his seven Tour de France medals for illegal doping, Armstrong was heralded for his perseverance, hyperfocus, self-control, and commitment to reaching his goal. When the cyclist was publicly vilified, Boyd refused to abandon Armstrong as a friend. As far as Boyd was concerned, public opinion had nothing to do with what he respected and liked about Armstrong: his commitment to a cause and his resilience. Fighting cancer, long-distance cycling and solitary confinement with the threat of torture test the limits of men and their dedication to their goals and missions. They both experienced physical pain and emotional setbacks, uncertainty, and deprivation. And they both had to have a singular goal and laser focus on that goal. These common experiences were enough to allow Boyd—and some of the other POWs—to look past Armstrong's failings. Although some of the POWs have expressed disappointment that Armstrong cheated to achieve his cycling record, they stopped short of dismissing all his accomplishments and personal fortitude.

This unlikely link between ancient philosophy, professional sports, and the otherworldly experience of being a POW is the key to understanding how the Hanoi Hilton prisoners created a culture of resilience and success under circumstances in which other men had suffered irreparable harm.

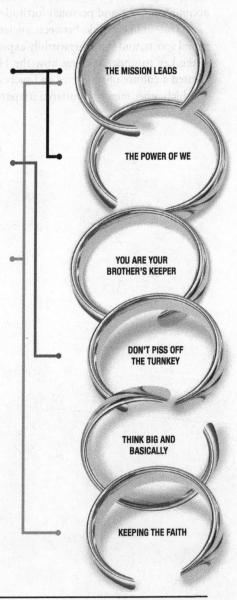

FIGURE 1.1 ~ The Rosetta Stone

The POWs' culture was hyperfocused on their mission. Before making a decision, they considered the question, "Does this move us toward achieving our mission?"

THE MISSION LEADS

The POWs' culture taught them to expend energy only on what they could control. For what they could control, they took full responsibility and offered no excuses. They learned to let go of what they could not control.

THE POWER OF WE

The POWs created a culture based largely on James Stockdale's understanding of the ancient philosophies of the Greek Stoic, Epictetus. These teachings were later expressed in sports psychology, performance enhancement, and psychological theories.

YOU ARE YOUR BROTHER'S KEEPER

DON'T PISS OFF THE TURNKEY

THINK BIG AND BASICALLY

KEEPING THE FAITH

CHAPTER 2

Lucky or Learned:
Looking for Resilience

On August 5, 1964, Everett Alvarez Jr., a young Navy pilot serving on board the USS *Constellation*, was startled awake by the phone shortly after 10 a.m. "Alvie, they want you in AI [Air Intercept]." The twenty-six-year-old aviator arrived in the briefing room to hear unexpected but, for a fighter pilot, thrilling news. He was going to be in the first group of U.S. fighter pilots to fly over North Vietnam. Two Navy ships, the USS *Turner Joy* and USS *Maddox*, reported that they had been torpedoed by the North Vietnamese in the Gulf of Tonkin. The United States was depicting the event as brazen, unprovoked aggression in international waters.

The truth was much murkier, but many politicians in Washington—and especially President Lyndon Johnson—were looking for an excuse to bomb North Vietnam. While eyewitness reports—including intelligence that disputed the attacks—were still being collected and analyzed, the president went on the airwaves to announce that "air action is now in execution against gunboats and certain supporting facilities in North Vietnam which have been used in these hostile operations." Alvarez and the nine other pilots ordered to make the strikes had not even arrived on target when the president effectively put the North Vietnamese on full alert.

The A-4 Skyhawks rendezvoused and headed for their bombing target—a naval base along the North Vietnam coast. Alvarez recalls feeling jittery, but not scared, about his first real combat mission. The ten pilots reached their target quickly, and Alvarez and his flight leader were the first two to descend on the naval base.

As Alvarez fired his rockets at four torpedo boats and a larger ship, they returned fire. He recalls the few moments it took for his world to change: hydraulic and fire alarm lights lit up, smoke filled the cockpit, and he battled to keep the plane under control while he ejected. Moments later, he hit the waters of the Gulf of Tonkin. Alvarez found himself in the unenviable position of becoming the first U.S. aviator captured and held in North Vietnam. Of course, the Gulf of Tonkin incident plunged the United States into nearly a decade of war, halfway around the world.

For nearly six months Alvarez was the only American aviator held in captivity in North Vietnam, and for much of that time, he was in solitary confinement. He does not recall being uncomfortable in isolation. Raised in a household with an alcoholic and abusive father, he says, "I think I found it easy because I had learned to live with myself. When you grow up in a turbulent household, you have to learn to shut things out. It was a mechanism for me, a survival technique."[1]

He coped in captivity by compartmentalizing his experiences and his feelings, distracting himself. He was used to being alone and could easily entertain and occupy himself for long stretches. This ability to set his emotions aside and put his predicament in perspective was something he brought with him—whether learned or innate, it was a survival technique that became handy in Vietnam.

MILITARY AVIATORS ARE WIRED DIFFERENTLY

Tucked away in the quiet confines of Naval Air Station Pensacola, the home of naval aviation, is a nondescript, one-story building that has been quietly and diligently tracking the physical and mental health of the Vietnam POWs for forty years. The Mitchell Center for POW Studies is named for retired Navy captain Robert E. Mitchell, a former Navy flight surgeon who spent more than fifteen years working at the U.S. Naval School of Aviation Medicine and the Naval Aerospace Medical Research Laboratory before taking the lead role in the medical evaluations of the returnees from Vietnam.

As early as 1971 the services had established the Center for POW Studies at Point Loma, in San Diego, California, in anticipation of the prisoners' release and a need to monitor their health. A few years later the other services shut down their formal programs. Mitchell and the Navy continued their program, and the Mitchell Center was born, under the Naval Operational Medicine Institute in Pensacola. Mitchell personally performed evaluations until 1990, when he retired.

The Mitchell Center pioneered the only longitudinal study of the long-term effects of the POW experience. Returnees are invited to Pensacola for an annual, complete medical evaluation courtesy of the Mitchell Center. Although the program is voluntary, many participate because of the quality of the care, their respect for the Mitchell Center's commitment to the well-being of all former POWs, and the knowledge that the data collected will benefit future generations of POWs and military service members.

Recognizing that the Vietnam POWs were predominantly aviators, the researchers at the Mitchell Center have asked the question: Did the aviator wings give the Vietnam POWs an extra edge over other POW populations? Did the training required to become a military aviator help them survive the POW experience? Or, was there a certain personality type attracted to military aviation that made them particularly well-suited for the POW experience?

Dr. Jeffrey Moore, at the Mitchell Center, set out to examine the unique qualities of the aviator personality, that ill-defined "right stuff" in their DNA that made them good aviators. Starting in 1993, Moore and his colleagues gave a personality research form (PRF) to 376 retired military aviator POWs with a mean age of fifty-eight. The objective of the study was to relate various personality traits to flight safety, combat effectiveness, aeronautical adaptability, aircrew coordination, and career achievement—and to evaluate the reproducibility of these traits for more effective recruitment and retention. But what the survey revealed was a profile of precisely the type of person you would want on your team when times are tough.

Titled "The Five As of Aviator Personality," the study identified five key components of a military aviator's core personality—a description of what you need to be the perfect POW: adventure, aggression, affiliation, achievement, and adaptability.[2]

HIGHLY COMPETITIVE, BUT TEAM PLAYERS

Moore explains, "This study implies that the core aviator personality has one unique personality trait—an uncommonly high correlation between a need for *affiliation* and *ambition*. They are achievement-oriented *and* highly affiliative."[3] In other words, they are ambitious, but not at the cost of their relationships to others; they are very team-oriented. So, the survey demonstrated that affiliation and ambition create an effective team player.

Moore notes that these two personality traits—affiliation and ambition—are polar opposites for most people. The combination of these two traits makes the difference in the aviators. Most high achievers are not inherent team players; the desire to be affiliated with people while thoroughly trouncing them in daily competition requires a delicate balance beyond the emotional intelligence of most people. (Both traits are quite easily measured with standard personality testing.)

Moore adds, "When the POWs were compared to an aviator (non-POW) control group, the control group was the same." In other words, aviators are aviators; the Hanoi Hilton aviators were basically the same as their peers who were not POWs.[4]

While it's unlikely that the military specifically recruited people with this unique combination of personality traits for their aviator ranks, the requirements to become an aviator probably attracted people with them. In contrast, the selection process for POWs was quite random. There was no way to predict which pilots would be shot down with a mathematical formula. And the POWs had no choice over whom their cellmates would be for up to nine years. They had to stay in the game with the hand they were dealt.

TOUGH LIFE EXPERIENCES SHAPED SUCCESS

Alvarez had a lot going for him when he was shot down. He résumé showed that he had earned an engineering degree from the University of Santa Clara, was commissioned as a naval officer, earned the gold wings and associated prowess of a trained naval aviator, and survived the lessons of Survival, Evasion, Resistance, and Escape (SERE) training. Even at age twenty-six, he was seasoned.

But he was about to become one of the longest-held U.S. POWs in history. When he returned home in 1973, he had spent nearly a quarter of his life in prison. And although his wife left him while he was held captive, he returned home, found love again, remarried, and raised two sons—a lawyer and a Navy doctor. Raised by poor Mexican immigrants, Alvarez left prison behind and became the epitome of the American dream. He has realized significant professional and personal success.

Alvarez has pursued a highly successful career—both in public service to every president since Reagan and as a serial entrepreneur, building several multimillion-dollar government contracting businesses. Was it nature or nurture? Was he born with the Teflon personality traits that gave him a buffer against the long-term effects of the trauma caused by the POW experience? Or did his military and aviation training, as well as the leadership of Stockdale and other SROs, make the difference and enable him to emerge from the experience practically unscathed?

What is unusual about Everett Alvarez's story is that his experience was not unique among his colleagues in captivity.

Most of the prisoners returned home physically and mentally intact, most of them later pursued highly successful careers in leadership positions, and few of them have exhibited long-term PTSD. Indeed, a study conducted on repatriated Navy POWs has shown cumulative incidence rates for PTSD of 4 percent.[5] This is much lower than the lifetime prevalence rate of 30.6 percent among a sample of male Vietnam-theater veterans who were surveyed as part of the National Vietnam Veterans Readjustment Study.

WIRED FOR RESILIENCE?

Researchers say that many factors—both internal and external—can affect a person's ability to weather trauma. And a growing body of research proves that most humans possess natural resiliency that enables them to rebound from traumatic events.

Dr. George Bonanno, a professor of psychology at Columbia University, has turned the traditional theory of grieving and trauma response on its head, challenging parts of the popular theories of Freud and Kubler-Ross on how humans deal with grief and tragedy. Bonanno has studied survivors of the September 11, 2001, attacks; the severe acute respiratory syndrome (SARS) epidemic in Asia; and childhood sexual abuse. He outlines four parallel trajectories of grief and asserts that only a small percentage of the population experiences chronic dysfunction or delayed grief as a result of a traumatic event. What if short-term PTSD symptoms—lasting three to six months after a traumatic event—were considered normal? What if these symptoms were considered part of the healing process, like a scab is to a wound?[6]

Alvarez is a perfect case study for Bonanno. His values were rooted in multiple generations of his family. Earnest and emotional about the adversities his maternal grandmother and parents faced throughout their lives, Alvarez says, "All three had missed out on so many of the joys of childhood due to the rigors of poverty. To make ends meet they had all been compelled prematurely to take on the responsibilities of adults. Family stories of the adversities they faced had shaped my character and given me backbone."[7]

Alvarez sees his family's poverty as a source of strength, not a source of future problems. That outlook—the ability to find the value in the hand dealt to you by life—was a hallmark of the POWs' attitude and perspective. Alvarez understood that he needed to help model that attitude for other pilots as they joined him in the Hanoi Hilton. "The best thing I did was just be there. The stories go that my cellmates used to say, 'I used to feel sorry for myself, but then I'd look at you.'"[8] Alvarez was a leader in the Hanoi Hilton simply because he had survived longer than the rest of them. He was the de facto role model just by being there. He felt he had an example to set for others, for the team of men who were in captivity with him. This obligation motivated and strengthened him.

BACK TO THE ANCIENT PHILOSOPHERS: THE CRITICAL POWER OF YOUR BELIEFS

More than any other factor, Alvarez's personal values (his belief system) were the lens through which he was able to translate his situation in captivity and put it in perspective. He expected adversity, but he also expected to survive. He wrote, "As I grew up, I began to sense the values that austerity had taught my grandmother and parents. Their collective legacy would never be measured in material worth. Instead it would be defined in terms of human endurance and the need to survive. Our lot was to struggle and to overcome. That was best done through hard work and education. The alternative meant yet another generation of vulnerability to low pay for unskilled labor."[9]

Dr. Albert Ellis, the author and first proponent of rational emotive behavior therapy (REBT), was one of the first scientists to recognize that people's interpretation of events determines their reaction to them. He said that his theory was based on ancient Asian philosophers, such as Confucius, Lao-tzu, and Gautama Buddha—as well as Epictetus, who "stated that people are disturbed not by things but by *their view of things* [italics added]."[10] A person's belief system is the key.

"Belief is immediately what you tell yourself about that situation (traumatic event). That belief system is like a lens that filters everything we experience. It develops ever since we were five years old on," explains Cdr. Eric Potterat, PhD, a Navy psychologist at the Naval Special Warfare Center in Coronado, California. Potterat has studied these issues for several years in his work recruiting and training Navy SEALs.

> Some developmental psychologists would disagree with me, but for the most part, we don't start developing personality until about the fourth or fifth year. So, every experience you have from year four or five on starts to hone that lens and contributes to stereotypes, biases, and prejudices. That's going to guide how I interpret every event from that point forward. So, when you examine meta-analytical research on belief systems, those individuals who are able to navigate through negative life events with rational, healthy stereotypes, biases, etc., will likely navigate the next adversity with a positive outcome. Those with an irrational belief system are more likely to continue using irrational beliefs and will more likely navigate adverse situations with a negative outcome.[11]

Ellis claimed that this belief system was inherent, biological. He did not believe that it was acquired over a lifetime. He wrote, "The REBT theory of acquisition can be summed up in the view that as humans we are not disturbed simply by our experiences; rather, we *bring our ability to disturb ourselves to our experiences* [italics added]."[12]

Potterat and other military researchers and clinicians have revisited Ellis' theories to hone their ability to recruit more resilient soldiers, sailors, and Marines. Like employers, they are looking for people who have rational belief systems. In the Hanoi Hilton, Stockdale interpreted the teachings of Epictetus and asked each POW to take responsibility for how they viewed their predicament. He asked them to adopt a rational belief system that focused on mission success.

YOUR CHOICES: COMMITMENT, CONTROL, AND CHALLENGE

Dr. Paul Bartone is a retired Army colonel and a psychologist at the Industrial College of the Armed Forces at the National Defense University in Washington, D.C. He uses the term "hardiness" to describe the type of personality that leads an individual to become more resilient in the face of stress. Much like Ellis, he narrows in on how individuals interpret events: "Hardy persons have a high sense of life and work *commitment*, a greater feeling of *control*, and are more open to change and *challenges* in life [italics added]. They tend to interpret stressful and painful experiences as a normal aspect of existence, part of life that is overall interesting and worthwhile."[13]

Alvarez's commitment to serving as a role model to his fellow POWs, his clear understanding of what he could control about his surroundings and predicament, and his willingness to take on the challenge of serving as that role model—all these factors contributed to his belief that he was going to make it. They provided intangible protection against the effects of extreme suffering and deprivation.

You get to choose whether you will commit and how much you will commit to challenges and obstacles that confront you. You get to decide whether to let go of what you cannot control and focus your energy on what you can control. You get to decide whether and how much you accept change and challenge in your life. Embrace those choices and life becomes, as Bartone puts it, "interesting and worthwhile." Shrink from those choices and life can become more "stressful and painful."

NATURE *AND* NURTURE

The debate over which matters most—nature or nurture—continues among scientists who research what makes individuals and organizations perform at high levels under difficult circumstances. The empirical data from the Hanoi Hilton suggests it was both nature and nurture that helped the POWs survive so well. Personal traits played a role, both in the POWs' success while in captivity and in their subsequent careers. But, the culture that was intentionally developed among the prisoners also played a large role in their survival and contributed to success later in their careers. The Hanoi Hilton was, in essence, an incubator in which high-performance teamwork became common.

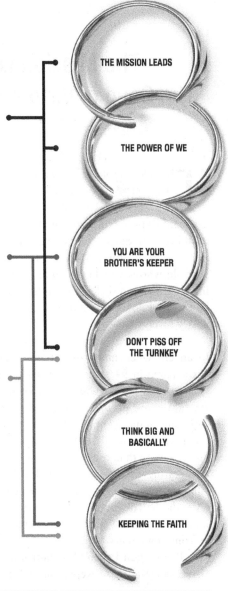

FIGURE 2.1 ~ Lucky or Learned

The Hanoi Hilton high-performance culture successfully blended competitiveness with teamwork. A prison full of striving achievers could have been plagued by widespread maverick behavior. But the unusual combination of high scores in achievement and high scores in affiliation (typified by a willingness to work with others and build a team) created a high-performance outcome. The process of reaching common ground was daunting, but the core members of this high-performance culture checked their egos at the door and found a way to work to achieve their mission.

The prisoners' high-performance culture consisted largely of mature people who had shown resilience and persistence in previous life experiences. Age was a benefit. They worked to spread behaviors and expectations that encouraged realism, optimism, and resilience in each other.

The prisoners' high-performance culture was dominated by rational belief systems. They approached their challenges and setbacks with a philosophy grounded in reality. They expected adversity, yet they also expected to survive and succeed against adversity. They rationally analyzed their problems, marshaled their resources, and focused their energies. Fear and other emotional responses did not dominate their thinking or drive their behavior.

THE MISSION LEADS

THE POWER OF WE

YOU ARE YOUR BROTHER'S KEEPER

DON'T PISS OFF THE TURNKEY

THINK BIG AND BASICALLY

KEEPING THE FAITH

CHAPTER 3

The Mission Leads:
The Seed of Virtual Leadership

The Honorable Sam Johnson has represented the Third District of Texas as a U.S. representative since 1991. He splits his time between the Dallas metropolitan area and Capitol Hill, traveling back and forth several times a month, and frequently works sixty-hour weeks. His schedule is not an easy one for a young man, much less for an eight-two-year-old who is wracked with arthritis and still suffers lingering muscular and skeletal wounds from injuries incurred when he was shot down over North Vietnam and held as a POW for nearly seven years.

Congressman Johnson has an impressive voting record. In an era when many of his colleagues miss votes, he has participated in 94 percent of votes arising during his time in Congress. In an era when many of his colleagues pander to special interest groups, he is known for standing by his principles and standing up for his convictions—regardless of their popularity. His loyal staff—many of whom have worked for him for more than a decade—frequently tell the story of their boss staring down a firing squad in North Vietnam as a tangible and visceral example of his tenacity and its origins. They relay the harrowing tale in its entirety—his shoot-down, his capture, the march north to the Hanoi Hilton, and the lineup in front of an angry mob.

But a factor beyond his control probably played as much a role as anything in Representative Johnson's surviving this incident. His captors did not want dead POWs on their hands; on the contrary, the POWs were one of the North Vietnamese's best bargaining chips throughout the war. But the sheer terror the incident caused could have forced a weaker man to give up information. The firing squad bluff could have been a powerful instrument of torture. But it didn't work on Sam Johnson.

He recounted the story of staring down three soldiers armed with rifles in his memoir, *Captive Warriors*: "I remember feeling as if I was suspended in time, as if I was standing outside my body and watching some macabre play. It wasn't happening! It couldn't be happening! Everything inside me rejected the hideous scene that played in front of me. Then through the fog of disbelief, a tiny piece of my brain skidded toward reality, and I said silently, 'Jesus, I love you.'"[1] Johnson was a deeply religious man, and this traumatic experience crystallized his faith. It helped him focus on what was important and what was going to give him purpose and meaning.

KEEPING PERSPECTIVE, STAYING FOCUSED

Many years later, in the summer of 2002, the Sarbanes-Oxley bill was being debated in Congress. One provision involved pension disclosure, an issue that was pertinent to two powerful House committees: the Ways and Means Committee and the Education and Workforce Committee. This meant that two powerful committee chairmen, Representative Bill Thomas of Ways and Means and Representative John Boehner of Education and Workforce, had jurisdiction over this issue.

According to former Johnson staffer and tax policy adviser Kathleen Black, "Thomas's committee is always described as 'the powerful Ways & Means Committee' and, befitting that, the Chairman considered it to be preemptive of any other Committee's interests. Further, members are sometimes beholden to the Chairman because it is also traditionally an *exclusive* Committee—their *only* committee assignment."[2]

Apparently, Congressman Johnson didn't agree with that tacit rule. He remains the only member of Congress to ever serve concurrently on both committees. Also, he was the Education and Workforce subcommittee chairman with jurisdiction over pensions, and he was particular about protecting his provision involving the Employee Retirement Income Security Act (ERISA), a federal law that sets minimum standards for pension plans in private industry. The issue at stake was a provision in the new law designed to prevent another Enron debacle. In that case, Enron had restricted its shareholders from selling company shares when bad news was breaking. Enron claimed it was making "management changes." The new provision required that thirty-day "blackout notices" be sent to 401(k) participants so employees would have fair warning that they would be prevented from making stock changes in their plan.

Black wrote that Chairman Thomas liked to hone his image as a tough power broker and thought that the Ways and Means Committee, not the subcommittee chairman, should be writing this provision and making this decision. Thomas would show Congressman Johnson who was boss.

So, Sam and I got called to the Chairman's Capitol office. It was not the historic Ways & Means room, but instead the Chairman's office on the first floor of the Capitol. It had swinging doors on it—like the western "OK Corral"—and because it was across the hall from the physician's office, the air had an odd medicinal odor. As we walked through the swinging doors, Thomas's counsel was standing in the entry room between two desks on the right, and Thomas was waiting for Sam in his office doorway at the end of the room on the left. The Congressman walked ahead of me and Thomas's staffer steps in front of me to cull me from the boss. When Sam got to Thomas, Thomas started yelling and the staffer started yelling at me. The Congressman wasn't even sitting down. He was just standing there—as straight as Sam can stand—looking at Thomas yelling at him. Shocked and indignant, my eyes were darting back and forth between the guy yelling at me and watching Sam getting yelled at. Rage was building in my chest as I was barely even listening to what was being said.

Finally, Thomas stopped long enough for the Congressman to get a word in edgewise. Sam just calmly asked, "Are you done yet?" Silence from Thomas. Sam turned on his heels, walked toward me, I fell in line behind him and we departed smartly through the swinging doors.

Black was in shock. She had never been yelled at like that in her career. And she was fuming that the staffer yelled in chorus with his boss. "As we're walking up the ramp past the physician's office, Sam saw that I was positively electric with anger. I'm pretty sure I was levitating at this point. If I had been a cat I'd have had a bottle brush tail sticking straight up with sparks emanating from it." But Congressman Johnson thought it was funny. "He started chuckling at me, and cuffed me with his arm that is all stiff from being beaten, and he asked if I was okay. I sputtered that I'd never been yelled at like that . . . and how dare Thomas yell at him, too!"[3]

At this point in their long walk back to the office across the street from the Capitol, Congressman Johnson stopped, looked Black in the eye, and said patiently in his signature, slow Texas drawl, "Ya know, the Vietnamese held me for seven years, Thomas can only be chairman for six." Black started laughing. "I knew then I was working for the greatest boss ever, who certainly wasn't going to back down because someone yelled at him."

She added as a footnote that his persistence paid off. Congressman Johnson's version of the bill got signed into law.[4]

The point is clear. Congressman Johnson has perspective, based on what he has survived in his life. But he is also willing to endure just about anything for his principles. He knew Congressman Thomas' reputation, he knew he was defying him, and he knew that he was in Thomas' crosshairs. When Thomas called him for a meeting, Johnson knew he was heading in for a proverbial beating. But it didn't matter. Johnson had confidence in his convictions, and he had a goal in mind from which he would not waver. A little tongue-lashing couldn't change his convictions. On the contrary, it sustained the congressman and further solidified his ideals, much like the firing squad.

FINDING A "WHY" IN LIFE: THE KEY TO HANDLING SUFFERING AND SETBACKS

In his best-selling and groundbreaking book on surviving the Holocaust, *Man's Search for Meaning*, psychoanalyst and Holocaust survivor Dr. Viktor Frankl managed to inspire generations of people from all walks of life by communicating a surprising lesson from his traumatic experience in a Nazi concentration camp. Frankl tapped into the deepest parts of the human soul and articulated the import suffering can bring to an ultimately fulfilling and fulfilled life. Indeed, as he articulated, "If there is a meaning in life at all, then there must be a meaning in suffering. Suffering is an ineradicable part of life, even as fate and death. Without suffering and death human life cannot be complete."[5]

What constitutes the meaning in life that Frankl describes? How did he muster hope and optimism in a concentration camp where he witnessed mass suffering and murder daily? Frankl outlines a method used to plumb meaning from the depths of the soul and how he used it to buoy himself—spiritually, intellectually, and even physically—over time. The method is closely related to the practice of setting goals.

Frankl writes, "The Latin word *finis* has two meanings: the *end* or the *finish*, and a *goal* to reach. A man who could not see the end of his *provisional existence* was not able to aim at an ultimate goal in life [italics added]." He then explains the importance of having a goal:

A man who lets himself decline because he could not see any future goal found himself occupied with retro-

THE MISSION LEADS 33

spective thoughts. . . . Instead of taking the camp's dif-
ficulties as a test of their inner strength, they did not
take their life seriously and despised it as something
of no consequence. They preferred to close their eyes
and to live in the past. Life for such people became
meaningless. . . . We could say that most men in a concentration camp believed that the real opportunities
of life had passed. Yet, in reality, there was an opportunity and a challenge. One could make a victory of
those experiences, turning life into an inner triumph,
or ignore the challenge and simply vegetate, as did a
majority of the prisoners.[6]

Having a goal, or meaning, in life became a central theme
in Frankl's writing about lessons he learned from his Holocaust
experience. He emphasized that each individual is responsible
for finding their meaning.

By declaring that man is responsible and must actual-
ize the potential meaning of his life, I wish to stress
that the true meaning of life is to be discovered in the
world rather than within man or his own psyche. . . .
It denotes the fact that being human always points,
and is directed, to something, or someone, other than
himself—be it a meaning to fulfill or another human
being to encounter. The more one forgets himself—by
giving himself to a cause to serve or another person to
love—the more human he is and the more he actual-
izes himself.[7]

Frankl spent his post–World War II career pioneering and
proselytizing this philosophy. He coined the term "logotherapy" as the therapeutic method or approach to this philosophy, which fundamentally believed that man can endure any
challenge or tragedy if he has defined and found this meaning,
or cause, in his life.

For most people, that intangible meaning in life translates
to faith in a religion, but not unanimously so. It can be a pur-

pose that is simply "larger than me." Frankl quoted Friedrich Nietzsche as saying, "He who has a *Why* to live can bear with almost any *How* [italics added]."[8]

FINDING PURPOSE IN THEIR MISSION

What logotherapy does not dictate is what that purpose is. For the POWs in the Hanoi Hilton, their purpose was translated into a simple mission that was commonly embraced and that addressed the unusual challenge facing them. Unlike other POW populations in other wars, members of this group felt like they were part of the war effort—despite being incarcerated. As Dr. Frederick Kiley and Dr. Stuart Rochester wrote in their definitive and encyclopedic accounting of the Vietnam POW experience, *Honor Bound*, "For them, the prison camps became just another theater, albeit a unique one, with its own peculiar logistical and tactical demands. Their mission had changed, from one of active fighting to one of resistance and survival, but they still had a soldierly function to perform—to disrupt, to stymie, to exhaust the enemy, finally to defeat him, in this case on the battlefield of propaganda and psychological warfare."[9]

Distributing propaganda and conducting psychological warfare are totally different from flying fighter jets and performing bombing missions over enemy territory. But for the early arrivals to the Hanoi Hilton and the identified leaders of the group—James Stockdale, Jeremiah Denton, and Robinson "Robbie" Risner—the establishment of a mission that could serve as their weapon in this unusual form of warfare was paramount. As Stockdale himself described it, "In Vietnam the American POW did not suddenly find himself on the war's sidelines. Rather, he found himself on one of the major battlefronts—the propaganda battlefront."[10]

And so Return with Honor was born. It was simple and clear. And, most importantly, it gave the men purpose. "Return with Honor" meant returning home from Vietnam without giving in to the enemy's attempts at psychological indoctrination—and betraying fellow POWs or the United States. It meant fighting and winning the war of propaganda.

~ The Role of Leaders in Building Resilience ~

Early in February 1967 James Stockdale experienced what he called his "first leadership crisis." His captors were requiring the POWs to read aloud *New York Times* articles that were critical of U.S. war efforts in Vietnam over the camp "squawk box," or loudspeakers. One POW assigned this punishment was clever enough to mispronounce some of the key words of the news story—effectively mocking his captors. His humorous resistance went unnoticed by the captors, provided some comic relief for the POWs, and boosted morale. But Stockdale was worried.

He recalled from a graduate school class on comparative Marxist thought that the North Koreans had effectively brainwashed American POWs by exploiting their need and desire to communicate with each other. During the Korean POW experience, skilled Communist Party representatives would assemble a group of POWs for "criticism/self-criticism sessions" during which the prisoners were encouraged to discuss and debate communist doctrine. Giving credence to communist propaganda through serious and thoughtful discussion did not by itself brainwash the POWs, but the tactic probably helped erode the POWs' willingness to stand together in that tense and fearful environment.

Stockdale reasoned that while the tap code communications tactic was a positive one, face-to-face communications and debate of this type—albeit through a radio—might not be so productive in an already emotionally daunting situation. If the articles began eroding the beliefs and commitment of a few POWs, the fragile unity he knew they must maintain to survive—the group's collective resilience—would erode.

Then another prisoner was asked to read more of these *New York Times* articles that seemed sympathetic to the Communists. This time, the narrator was more serious—and perhaps ponderous—about the content he was reading. Stockdale was so bothered by the subtle trajectory he was witnessing, he was moved to act. He ordered all the POWs to refuse to speak on the camp radio. The next five men who were asked refused. Those who had performed the duty before and who now refused were punished with several days of confinement in leg irons. But no one was ever asked to go on the camp radio again.

(continued)

Stockdale writes of the lesson learned: "Unified prison commitment, clearly perceived by the Vietnamese before they had been able to get a significant number on the hook, could win. . . . In short, unity was our best hope. And in our prison unity came automatically."[1]

Stockdale knew his men and knew what they were made of: they were all aviators with most of the same skills, trained in the same professional discipline. But he also knew that they "wanted above all else to enter a society of peers that had rules putting some criteria of right and wrong into their lives." Stockdale knew instinctively what many psychologists theorize: leaders maintain unity of purpose by maintaining commitment to and belief in the mission. When times are tough, nothing does that as well as clear instructions from the leader that point directly toward the commonly held mission. In this case, when Stockdale spotted the potential damage of the loudspeaker reading sessions, he refocused his men on their mission, Return with Honor, at the tactical level. The ramifications for the organization were monumental. A leader like Stockdale helps shape the experience of individuals under his command. This involves articulating the mission and giving team members specific instructions for resisting efforts to erode their beliefs and commitment to their mission.

It would seem natural that a peer or a leader has this ability to influence his or her teammates. But many scientists suggest that leaders who are resilient themselves can best effect resilience in an organization. Army psychologist Dr. Paul Bartone asserts, "If a stressful or painful experience can be cognitively framed and made sense of within a broader perspective that holds that all of existence is essentially interesting, worthwhile, fun, a matter of personal choice, and providing chances to learn and grow, then the stressful experience can have beneficial psychological effects instead of harmful ones."[2]

Sam Johnson, a cellmate of Stockdale's, recounts seeing Stockdale emerge from solitary confinement one time: "The serene strength that had characterized him when I first met him was gone. In its place were fear and such absolute sadness that it was almost a physical presence in the cell." Johnson recalls that over the next few weeks, Stockdale started "squaring his shoulders," and "the crisp solid commander's stance" returned. Stockdale soon resumed his role of setting the pace for the POWs' performance.[3]

[1] James B. Stockdale and Sybil Stockdale, *In Love and War: The Story of a Family's Ordeal and Sacrifice During the Vietnam Years* (New York: Harper & Row, 1984), 246–47.
[2] Paul T. Bartone, "To Build Resilience: Leader Influence on Mental Hardiness," *Defense Horizons*, November 2009, 141.
[3] Stuart I. Rochester and Frederick T. Kiley, *Honor Bound: American Prisoners of War in Southeast Asia, 1961–1973* (Annapolis, MD: U.S. Naval Institute Press, 1999), 517.

In the 1998 PBS documentary *Return with Honor*, POW Jerry Singleton spoke on the importance of this mission: "The motto, decided upon by our senior leaders was, *Return with Honor*. Returning by itself, without honor, was not going to be satisfactory. Having the honor but never returning would be something short of what our ultimate goal was."[11]

The organization created and maintained by the living former POWs, NAM-POWs, Inc., has a stated purpose on its website:

> Of the 800 Southeast Asia POWs, 470 were tortured and imprisoned in North Vietnam, some longer than eight years, 262 were in South Vietnam jungle POW camps for as long as nine years, thirty-two were in Laos, thirty-one in Cambodia and five in China (three of whom were held for over eighteen years under sub-human conditions). We are missing the membership of some 235 who left the armed services upon their return, blended into the workforce, and have not yet joined our ranks. We are finding them one by one, and we welcome them into one of the strongest fraternal organizations in the world today. Today, we are bonded together, not by rank or by service, but by the deep knowledge and faith that we were one unit, one entity that the enemy could not destroy. We held our heads high with pride as we served our nation as Prisoners of War. We accomplished our sworn goal. We Returned With Honor.[12]

If other factors critical to a healthy culture are present in an organization, a bigger-than-life challenge will focus organizational purpose. Instead of competing with each other for the morsels, individuals with a singular organizational focus will collaborate in pursuit of a goal larger than their individual needs and differences. Return with Honor was just such a goal.

FIGURE 3.1 ~ The Mission Leads

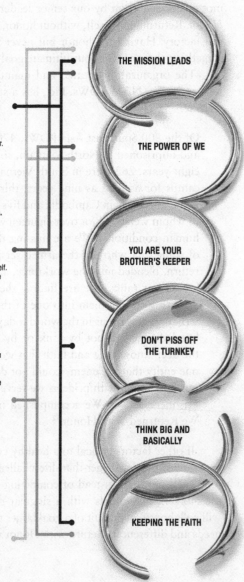

They developed laser focus on achieving this mission. Representative Sam Johnson knew he was going to take a beating for staking out his position against Representative Bill Thomas. He focused his energy on getting the bill passed the way he believed it should be passed. He did not spend energy on avoiding the beating, on resenting Thomas, or on evening the score later. He simply focused on succeeding at his mission.

THE MISSION LEADS

The Hanoi Hilton POWs believed in something bigger than themselves. Each found something that gave meaning to his plight: his faith, his family, his country, his organization's legacy, the person alongside him striving for the same goal, or his own image of how he wanted to see himself. These deep convictions sustained the prisoners through tough times.

THE POWER OF WE

YOU ARE YOUR BROTHER'S KEEPER

Their culture did not shrink from suffering, sacrifice, or pain. Every POW came to understand that success would bring scars. Their pain and suffering had purpose because they believed in their mission. They chose not to frame their circumstance as hopeless or themselves as helpless. Their experience left scars but, more importantly, built confidence. Representative Johnson knew that a tongue-lashing from Representative Thomas was inconsequential compared with his POW experiences. His Hanoi Hilton captors could have taken his life. His scars gave him confidence, not fear.

DON'T PISS OFF THE TURNKEY

THINK BIG AND BASICALLY

The POWs had a simple, clear mission. Most of them agreed that their singular focus was to "Return with Honor." They were expected to devote their energies and resources toward achieving that mission.

KEEPING THE FAITH

CHAPTER 4

You Are Your Brother's Keeper: The Catalyst for Virtual Leadership

The American bombing over North Vietnam resumed with ferocity in the fall of 1972, when the Paris peace talks broke down and President Nixon ordered Operation Linebacker, the campaign name for the first continuous bombing effort conducted against North Vietnam since President Johnson had halted bombing in late 1968. Operation Linebacker was intended to inhibit the transportation of supplies and materials by the North Vietnamese. The increased bombing runs over North Vietnam in the fall of 1972 resulted in more aviator shoot-downs and more POWs. By the end of 1972 a whole new group of aviators was joining the ranks of the old-timers.

They looked at men like Everett Alvarez and James Stockdale and wondered if they too would face a long incarceration. What did their future hold? How long would this seemingly intractable war continue? Although the increased bombing was encouraging to the old-timers, who believed that the effort would bring the North Vietnamese to the negotiation table, the prospects for release were no higher than they had been prior to the start of Linebacker. It was depressing.

FINDING PURPOSE IN PROTECTING THE GUY NEXT DOOR

Stockdale understood that this uncertainty could be their undoing. He later told of the relayed tap code messages he sometimes received from the "new guys." A pilot would ask, "I've got to have something to hang on to. What do you think I should hold as my highest value in here?" Stockdale said his reply was always, "The guy next door. Protect him. Love him. He is precious. He is your only link with our prison civilization in here."[1]

Stockdale also intuited that the military hierarchy—or chain of command—was not sufficient for the POW organization's goals in the Hanoi Hilton. His job was to ensure that his charges survived with their individual and organizational honor intact, that they had a goal to reach for and a mission to execute. To achieve that goal, he needed a different philosophy and approach. He needed to remind everyone—old-timers and new shoot-downs—to take care of his neighbor, the "guy next door."

Sam Johnson remembered the guidance and internalized it:

> Within a few days of our arrival at Las Vegas [a nick-name the POWs gave to one section of the Hanoi Hilton], [James] Lamar and I figured out that the large room next to ours was a holding tank for new prisoners. We knew there was a guy in there, but he would not respond to our efforts to communicate. During the guards' siesta I stood at the back window and yelled toward him, thinking he would get up and go to the window and talk to me, and I could tell him about the tap code. I had to get him into the system so we could get some encouragement to him. He had probably been beaten, maybe tortured with the ropes. We had to let him know someone cared. We had to break into his isolation. I remembered my first few hours in Heartbreak Hotel [the nickname for another section of the Hanoi Hilton], when Stockdale and Denton had called out to me and refused to let me give in to the desolation I felt. I had to do the same thing for this man.[2]

CELLMATES FOR MONTHS, BROTHERS FOR LIFE

Combat veterans frequently cite their battlefield motivation as limited to the man to the left and the man to the right. It is a simple survival strategy that has been time tested. In the case of the POWs, there were many stories of cellmates taking care of each other—nursing each other back to health, providing that emotional succor that boosted spirits when one was more depressed than the other. But one story of cellmate bonding stands out: the story of Porter Halyburton and Fred Cherry.

On the surface, the POWs had more in common with each other than they had differences. Most of them were white, college-educated, and highly trained as military officers and as aviators. They came from diverse socioeconomic backgrounds, but their commonalities gave them a foundation of homogeneity that helped them to overcome any differences. As a result of their racial and cultural differences, however, the process for Halyburton and Cherry took a bit longer. You see, Halyburton was a white man raised in the Jim Crow South and Cherry was a black man raised in the Jim Crow South.

They were thrown together in the same cell by the North Vietnamese, who were keenly aware of their racial differences and what that meant in American culture in the 1960s. Indeed, the North Vietnamese were hoping this forced, close-quarter coexistence would cause strife. And, while Halyburton and Cherry were initially wary of each other, the friendship and bond that developed between these two dissimilar men became legendary.

In a book written about them, *Two Souls Indivisible,* author James S. Hirsch describes their first meeting: "Having spent three weeks in dark, isolated rooms, [Halyburton] suddenly had contact with another human being. Close to a breakdown, desperate to talk to anyone, he was grateful to see Fred Cherry. But he was soon puzzled."[3] Halyburton, a Navy pilot, had no doubt Cherry was an American POW, but he was doubtful when Cherry said he was an Air Force pilot who flew F-105s. He had never met a black pilot and wasn't sure the Air Force had any. When Cherry told Halyburton that he was a major (two ranks above him), Halyburton was even more skeptical.

Likewise, Cherry had his guard up about Halyburton: "He didn't believe that [Halyburton] was a Navy lieutenant. He figured the Vietnamese would try anything to make him talk, so he thought Halyburton was a Frenchman spying for his captors. Halyburton didn't say or do anything to suggest such an identity; but Cherry's experience at survival schools had prepared him for Vietnamese duplicity, and he knew about the French colonialism in Indochina. It made sense to him that his handsome roommate would be a French spook, whose southern accent was one more clever ploy to throw him off the scent."[4]

A delicate dance of trepidation ensued between the two men, each testing the other out to validate his claims. When they finally learned that they had been shot down within five days of each other, they let their collective guards down. Slowly, over time, they began to trust each other. And Halyburton saved Cherry's life.

Cherry underwent three primitive surgeries to attempt to repair the shoulder he had shattered when he was shot down. Either because his surgeons were inept or because they didn't care about his fate—or both—Cherry suffered mightily. The first surgery produced few results, and the cast the doctors encased him in was too tight to foster healing. He was barely able to breathe, much less move. Halyburton became his cell-mate's nurse, helping him go to the bathroom, eat, and rehabilitate. According to Hirsch, "Halyburton feared that inactivity would cause Cherry to wither away, so he wanted his roommate to exercise. 'You have to walk to get your strength,' he said. 'Oh, Haly, I can't.' And he couldn't, at least not by himself. So he draped his right arm around Halyburton, leaned against him, and the two inched their way around the cell. . . . They had walked for only a few minutes when Cherry, exhausted, grabbed Halyburton, who caught him and carried him back to his bunk, like a soldier leaving a battlefield who would not leave his buddy behind."[5]

The seven and a half months Halyburton and Cherry spent together in that cell were but a small portion of their overall time in captivity—less than 10 percent. But it changed their whole outlook on the prison experience and their collective mission while in captivity. Hirsch writes, "They had been forced to live in a world different from any they had ever known. That world was harsh, but it also had a pureness and clarity of purpose. Survival transcended all other concerns, and traditional sources of tension—race, service, rank, family background—were replaced by the bonds of compassion and sacrifice."[6]

THE SERVANT LEADER: WALKING YOUR TALK

But what about the man who is in charge of these men? In the absence of imminent death and combat, how does a leader inspire that kind of care and sacrifice in pursuit of the collective mission?

Years after his release, Stockdale gave a speech in which he succinctly summarized his view on this subject:

> From this eight-year experience, I distilled one all-purpose idea. . . . It is a simple idea, an idea as old as the Scriptures, an idea that is the epitome of high-mindedness, an idea that naturally and spontaneously comes to men under pressure.
>
> If the pressure is intense enough or of long enough duration, this idea spreads without even the need for enunciation. It just takes root naturally. It is an idea that, in this big easy world of yackety yak, seems to violate the rules of *game theory*, if not of reason. It violates the idea of Adam Smith's invisible hand, our ideas of human nature, and the second law of thermodynamics. That idea is that *you are your brother's keeper*. [Italics added.][7]

Academics call this concept "servant leadership," a term coined by Robert K. Greenleaf in "The Servant as Leader," an essay that he first published in 1970. In that essay, he wrote,

> The servant-leader is servant first. . . . It begins with the natural feeling that one wants to serve, to serve first. Then conscious choice brings one to aspire to lead. That person is sharply different from one who is leader first, perhaps because of the need to assuage an unusual power drive or to acquire material possessions. . . . The leader-first and the servant-first are two extreme types. Between them there are shadings and blends that are part of the infinite variety of human nature.
>
> The difference manifests itself in the care taken by the servant-first to make sure that other people's highest priority needs are being served. The best test, and difficult to administer, is: Do those served grow as persons? Do they, while being served, become healthier, wiser, freer, more autonomous, more likely themselves to become servants? And, what is the effect on the least privileged in society? Will they benefit or at least not be further deprived?[8]

This type of proverbial "feet washing" was routinely practiced by the POWs in an effort to buoy each other's spirits when they were depressed, but more often it was used to recover from torture. "Although our leaders were often tortured first and most, they did not pretend to be macho 'John Wayne' heroes," says Vietnam POW Lee Ellis. "On the contrary, they openly shared the pain and despair of their brokenness, helping us understand the enemy's tactics and the realities of what was and was not possible. It would have been disastrous for the mission and for their credibility had they been less than totally honest with us about their experiences in the torture chambers. Mutual accountability and transparency in the face of a cruel enemy bonded us tightly together."[9]

While this openness and honesty had benefits for the more junior POWs and provided an example for them to follow, it also had healing powers for the leaders. According to Risner,

> Sometimes it really hurt to be honest, but the longer we were there, the more we appreciated it because it helped everybody. I've heard men come back saying, "Boy, I spilled my guts." . . . We said, "Don't sweat it. Most of the rest of us have been through the same thing. Let us brief you and tell you how things are going to go. You'll get your guts back in no time." By telling him what had happened to us, we knew he could put the information he had given in perspective and balance. That way he didn't figure he was the sole one giving information or that he had become a traitor because he was not strong enough to take torture to death.[10]

~ Finding Your Balance ~

Great leaders and great organizations actively work to achieve balance and perspective. Author Jim Collins first noted the balance brought to the POWs' culture by James Stockdale. In his best-selling book *Good to Great*, Collins called it "the Stockdale Paradox." Stockdale understood that two groups of POWs were at risk: those who were overly optimistic ("We'll be out by Christmas!") and those who had lost hope ("We will never get out alive.").

The prisoners desperately needed to believe that they would prevail. But they also needed brutal honesty about their current plight. They would get out, but not by Christmas. (Stockdale's wife, Sybil, recalls in their memoir *In Love and War* her dread when he wrote to her in 1971, six years after his capture, that he would not be home "for this Christmas, or for the next.")[1]

By balancing faith and optimism with brutal honesty about their dire straits, Stockdale positioned the Hanoi Hilton inmates to do the seemingly impossible: to defeat their captors' attempts to use them for propaganda and to return home as a team, without abandoning each other or their values. In finding organizational balance—which encouraged personal balance—between brutal honesty and

(continued)

unfailing faith in their ability to endure, the POWs survived up to nine years of deprivation, isolation, and torture and returned home with their heads held high. Great organizations learn to balance concepts and needs that are in tension. Navy SEALs put this principle in action routinely.

The psychologist for the Navy SEALs, Dr. Eric Potterat, asserts that biological factors account for much of the success of a Navy SEAL. In the nature versus nurture debate, he leans more toward the nature side of the argument—that SEALs are born with the ability to become a Navy SEAL. He has devoted much of his professional career to seeking ways to effectively screen for the biological and psychological traits that mattered to success in Basic Underwater Demolition school (BUD/S) training. He states, "If I had to assign a weighting, I would say it's 60 percent nature and 40 percent nurture. That said, I do believe that the 40 percent nurture is significant and can be developed and trained."[2]

However, Lt. Cdr. Josh Butner, the director of professional military education at the Naval Special Warfare Center, is convinced that success for SEALs is "all above the neck." He believes most of what the SEALs have achieved has been through mental toughness. He pointed out that every candidate that walks through the door is already a top physical specimen—many of them star athletes. But two-thirds of them wash out during the training.[3]

Part of Butner's mission is to cultivate the mental toughness that he believes leads to SEAL success. Ironically, the ardent believer in nature over nurture, Potterat, is responsible for developing the robust mental toughness curriculum that Lieutenant Commander Butner embraced and administered with Potterat and the Naval Special Warfare Center staff. They have taught prospective Navy SEALs how to control their stress reactions, how to self-talk, how to visualize the process of achieving their goal while "eating the elephant one bite at a time," and how to set their goals and focus their energies on them. These concepts point to balance. You must strive for your long-range, overarching goal, but day to day, you must take each step individually and focus only on it.

It is precisely in the inherent tension created by two opposing beliefs—fervently held in the same organization—that greatness can flourish. The psychologist screens for biological traits, while the educator trains to improve as many environmental issues as possible. When the approaches are in balance, greatness develops.

---

[1] James B. Stockdale and Sybil Stockdale, *In Love and War: The Story of a Family's Ordeal and Sacrifice During the Vietnam Years* (New York: Harper & Row, 1984), 391.
[2] Eric G. Potterat, interview by the authors, August 19, 2010.
[3] Josh Butner, interview by the authors, August 19, 2010.

The value of that immediate debrief in lifting the spirits of fellow POWs could not be overestimated. Stockdale often told a story of a fellow POW who did post-captivity graduate research on whether torture or isolation was more effective when coercing information from a person; he surveyed a number of Hanoi Hilton survivors who had endured long stretches of both. Those who had endured the longest stretches of both torture and isolation considered isolation worse than torture. Stockdale noted, "From my viewpoint, you can get used to repeated rope torture—there are some tricks for minimizing your losses in that game. But keep a man, even a very strong-willed man, in isolation for three or more years, and he starts looking for a friend, any friend, regardless of nationality or ideology."[11]

When leaders model a commitment to the organization, the individual, and the cause, their people will follow. This mind-set often requires counterintuitive humility and "others-oriented" thinking. Leaders like Stockdale, Denton, and Risner perfected this behavior. Academic and scientific experts have identified how they did it.

WHEN THINGS GET TOUGH: WHAT LEADERS NEED TO PROVIDE

At the Summa–Kent State University Center for the Treatment and Study of Traumatic Stress in Akron, Ohio, Dr. Stephen Hobfall is one of a handful of experts who is studying the role and impact of intervention after traumatic events, a type of "psychological first aid" that the POWs perfected—albeit with the encouragement of their leaders.

Dr. Hobfall outlines five essential elements of intervention that can mitigate the long-term impact of trauma: safety, optimism, calm, connectedness, and efficacy. Hobfall's research was more focused on aiding those affected by mass trauma, but he says that his findings have also proven helpful to combat veterans.[12] The five elements of intervention were critical in helping the POWs bounce back from bouts of depression, from torturous interrogation sessions, and from long stints of isolation. The intervention the POWs practiced provided them with a sense of security after a disorienting experience (torture or isolation); it was an attempt to provide hope again to an individual whose optimism had been shattered; it was a method to quiet and soothe a potentially delirious man; it reconnected the individual with the group; and it gave all POWs a sense of purpose and helped them overcome feelings of helplessness.

Dr. Hobfall focused his research on the immediate aftermath of a traumatic event under the assumption that the standard psychological debriefing was inadequate in preventing long-term PTSD. The POWs had learned this firsthand.

Fast-forward to September 2001. Federal Trade Commissioner Orson Swindle found himself in a unique position. He was one of five commissioners whose pledged duty was to protect the American consumers. He had earned his organization's respect with his decisiveness, convictions, and experience. But little of that mattered in those first few days after the 9/11 attacks. The Federal Trade Commission (FTC), like most organizations in the days immediately following the terrorist attacks, was reeling with horror, sadness, uncertainty, fear, and helplessness. Commissioner Swindle, who was at the time a leader by virtue of his appointment as a commissioner, sent an unsolicited e-mail to the entire organization. He solidified his place as a leader that day by modeling his values and quickly intervening when the FTC was paralyzed by trauma. His memo is a distillation of many of the principles the POWs learned and practiced in the Hanoi Hilton. Remember the initial days after September 11, 2001, and Commissioner Swindle's words will resonate as a wise and rational prescription for the uncertainty and unknown problems we suddenly understood that the United States faced.

Commissioner Swindle had remembered the simple credo from his years in captivity: You are your brother's keeper.

To:	ALL STAFF
From:	Orson Swindle III
Date:	Tuesday, September 18, 2001 1:22 PM
Subject:	Some thoughts on our tragedy

Thanks to Chairman Muris for his remarks to us all yesterday.

Indeed, we have all been stunned by the tragedies of this past week. The trauma continues as rescue and recovery operations go forth. We see anguish in the faces of those heroic men and women trying to help, and, of course, the grieving families, friends and our fellow workers. Several have asked me for my thoughts, given some of the experiences in my past.

First, let me assure you that nothing prepares any of us for this kind of tragedy. Marines cry, too, and I have shed a thousand tears this past week . . . and no doubt there are more to come. Just as you, I know some who have perished, either personally or by someone I know. We grieve. We ache. We fear. All of these emotions rack our minds and bodies and will affect our everyday activities from that tragic moment forward. No one will ever forget where we were, who we knew, what we felt on September 11, 2001.

But, as time passes, the silent moments of pain, anguish and tears will give way slowly to what we must do. We must carry on. We must and will get back to our everyday lives working professionally, loving our children, our families, friends, and our fellow coworkers and citizens, serving our nation and its wonderful people, and looking to the future. We must do these things.

We all, quite naturally, sense great fear arising from the attacks in New York and just across the Potomac. I am no stranger to fear. Together, we can handle fear.

There is debate as to what the President should do, and what should the Country do. Is war the answer? War is a terrible thought to us, especially those of us have experienced it firsthand.

Let me suggest that we not get too confused in the debate about what caused this and who is responsible. Too many are playing the blame game right now. From what I know and have observed over the years, I believe I can say what this tragedy is not. It is not gross negligence on the part of Americans who live in a free society. It is not something we sought. It is not racial conflict. It is not an ethnic or religious war between the good people of Islamic beliefs, or the good people of Palestine or Afghanistan and Christians, Jews, or Americans.

The tragedies we have witnessed are the heinous acts of madmen who represent very few people other than more madmen. To associate their acts with any people, nationality, race or religion is wrong, and we must not allow that to happen. And, no injustices of the past to anyone by anyone can be sufficiently rationalized to justify such murderous acts. Those who would bring this death, destruction, pain and suffering to innocent people represent no one and nothing other than insanity.

As to fear, let me suggest you get mad; that you become calmly enraged at those who would threaten and harm us. Fear, most often, overpowers and weakens. We should be enraged by these acts. That rage must continue. It drives away fear. We, as a people, detest intimidation, threats and violence to ourselves and our neighbors. We have been violated. We have been robbed of precious lives, of happy tomorrows, of smiling faces, of achievements to come by bright young people, of beautiful children yet to be, and of pleasant days at the end of successful lives. Good people of all ethnic, racial and religious origins from over 60 countries have died or are missing in New York. I take that personally. I am angry. I am enraged. I will not forget.

What must we do? We must rationally, logically, calmly, and professionally go about our lives now. We here at the FTC must get back to doing the great work that we do, being the pros that we are. We owe that to those we have lost and those who suffer. Our President and his civilian and military advisors will sort through it all, find the best answers for bringing those responsible to accountability, and we will do it. I believe we can be assured of that. We indeed are engaged now in a long conflict. We will be personally involved as few today can comprehend, but the Greatest Generation, our parents and grandparents, did it well and so will we. Stay strong and brave, and keep the faith.

We have work to do.

John Stuart Mill (1806–1873), British philosopher, expressing his opposition to England's siding with the Confederacy during our Civil War, said, "War is an ugly thing, but not the ugliest of things: the decayed and degraded state of moral and patriotic feeling which thinks nothing worth a war, is worse. . . . A war to protect other human beings against tyrannical injustice; a war to give victory to their own ideas of right and good, and which is their own war, carried on for an honest purpose by their own free choice—is often the means of their regeneration."

We can do this . . . and we will. God Bless . . .

Orson

Courtesy of Orson Swindle

FIGURE 4.1 ~ You Are Your Brother's Keeper

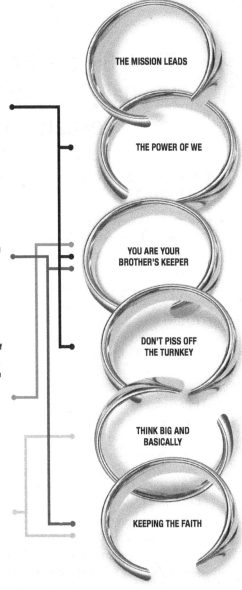

Their culture emphasized communication that fostered openness, honesty, connectedness, a sense of efficacy, and mutual support. Although isolation motivated the men to communicate, they faced two huge handicaps: certain punishment if they were caught and the lowest-tech methods imaginable for communicating. Despite these handicaps, they understood the critical role communication played in achieving mission success.

They balanced personal responsibility with a "brother's keeper" mentality. There was very little "I did my job, let him do his" indifference. Although the act of stopping to help somebody else could have conflicted with their culture's equally strong concept of personal responsibility, the POWs fostered caretaking as an integral part of thier mission. They practiced servant leadership.

The Hanoi Hilton POWs took care of their most important resource: their human resource. With virtually no tools other than each other and tin drinking cups to help them hear muffled taps on their cell walls, their mission was accomplished entirely with human performance and human interaction. This high-performance team consciously placed its human resources at the top of the list of its most important assets.

Their culture emphasized trusting that the other prisoners would do the right thing. It was essential that all POWs trusted and expected the others to grow to reflect the group's cultural norms in their behaviors.

THE MISSION LEADS

THE POWER OF WE

YOU ARE YOUR BROTHER'S KEEPER

DON'T PISS OFF THE TURNKEY

THINK BIG AND BASICALLY

KEEPING THE FAITH

CHAPTER 5

Think Big and Basically:
The Daily Map for Virtual
Leadership

James Stockdale recalled two crucial meetings during his earliest days as a POW:

After weeks in prison the man in charge of the prison camps took note of my refusal to make a statement critical of the United States and set me straight on priorities.

"You have a medical problem and a political problem. Politics comes before medicine in the DRV [Democratic Republic of Vietnam]. You fix the political problem in your head first, and then we'll see the doctors." The leg was never fixed.

I'll never forget my Christmas Day conversation with that senior Vietnamese officer, three months after I had been shot down in September, 1965. He said, "You are my age, and you and I share the military profession, and we have sons the same age, but there is a wall between us. The wall is there because we come from different social and political systems. But you and I must try to see through that wall and together bring this imperialist war of American aggression to an end. We know how to do this, but you must help me, you must influence the other American prisoners. Through propaganda [not a "bad word" in communist circles], we will win the war on the streets of New

52

York. All I ask is that you be reasonable. You will help me. You don't know it yet, but you will."

A week later I heard the church bells of Hanoi ring in the New Year 1966 at midnight. I was shivering without a blanket, legs in stocks, hands in cuffs, lying in three days of my own excrement. That was only the beginning. I became immersed in a system of isolation, of extortion, of torture, of silence.

Any American who from his solitary cell was caught communicating with another American, by wall tap, by whisper, you name it, was put back in the meat grinder to go from torture to submission to confession to apology to atonement.

That was a hard life, but I'm proud to say that torture became about the only route to propaganda for them because we met the challenge by communicating and taking lumps, by organizing, by resisting in unison, by giving them nothing free, making them hurt us before we gave an inch, by fighting "city hall."[1]

Organize, communicate, unite, fight—these verbs define any high-performance team that encounters opposition or competition. The need for a game plan—rules of the road—is obvious.

The demand for rules to live by came from the bottom up, Stockdale recalled. "On the parade ground, all the rankers [climbers trying to achieve status and rank] vie for leadership, to be out front; but in political prison, being the boss means you're the first guy down the torture chute when the inevitable purge starts. In that place, the drive for discipline and organization starts at the bottom and works its ways up. Maybe it always does when lives and reputations are at stake."[2]

Stockdale described the process that moved from cell to cell: "At least half of those wonderful competitive fly boys I found myself locked up with [said things like]: 'We are in a spot like we've never been in before. But we deserve to maintain our self-respect, to have the feeling we are fighting back.

We can't refuse to do every degrading thing they demand of us, but it's up to you, boss, to pick out the things we must all refuse to do unless and until they put us through the ropes again. Give us the list; what are we to take torture for?"[3]

KEEP THE GUIDELINES SIMPLE AND FOCUSED ON THE MISSION

In coming up with his response to the POWs' request, Stockdale relied on a principle he learned when a famed test pilot told him to forget memorizing checklists for restarting an engine in flight. The pilot told him he needed only three things when an engine died in midflight: air (get the nose down), fuel (pump some to the engine), and fire (get some sparks going). "Think big and basically and don't get rattled, and you'll live forever," the test pilot told Stockdale.[4]

Stockdale was faced with a Gordian knot. He wrote, "I put a lot of thought into what those first orders should be. My mind-set was 'we here under the gun are the experts . . . throw out the book and write your own.' My orders came out as easy-to-remember acronyms. The principal one was BACK-US."[5]

This acronym that Stockdale devised, BACK-US, laid down rules to guide daily life in prison. The rules were simple and clear, and every POW was expected to live them out to the best of their ability:

B meant "Don't Bow in Public." The prisoners were required to bow to the prison guards, and bowing to the guards in front of outsiders (visiting reporters, Red Cross representatives, etc.) became a propaganda tool for the captors. The prisoner would take a beating if he opted not to bow. Stockdale asked his followers to take the beating instead of giving their captors ammunition by prostrating themselves in public. In the privacy of their cells, POWs could bow rather than take a beating. Several, however, chose the beating. In this rule, Stockdale's expectations were balanced with some personal choice. In the privacy of their cells, the men could choose whether to bow or take a beating because only one hide was on the line. In public, bowing put the group's well-being in danger. There, personal interests took a backseat.

A stood for "Stay Off the Air." POWs were not to make any statements that the captors could broadcast across the camp, across Hanoi, or around the world. They were expected to put the interests of the group over their own self-interest.

C reminded the POWs that they should "Admit No Crimes." The POWs were constantly called war criminals (subject to prosecution, punishment, and even execution), not prisoners of war (protected by the Geneva Convention from torture and mistreatment and to be granted decent treatment, food, and medical care). The cultural expectation in this rule was clear: do not lend weight to a propaganda claim that could directly harm the rest of the prisoners and how they were viewed and treated.

K cautioned "Never Kiss Them Good-bye." In other words, don't ever show gratitude or goodwill toward the enemy. Stay focused on resisting and beating them at their own game. The cultural expectation here was that resistance was the norm. Accepting special treatment as an individual could drive a wedge into group unity and a mission-focused team. The POWs often disagreed about what constituted a favor and how far they should go to minimize conflict with their captors. Individual judgment varied. More importantly, room for personal judgment was routinely allowed, unless a POW was clearly jeopardizing others with his behavior.

US stood for both "United States" and, more importantly, "Unity over Self." This simple idea—that the group mission overrode self-interest—was the overarching principle that Stockdale wanted to supersede all other rules. It was the supreme guide to daily behavior.[6]

These were not policies in the usual corporate sense of the word. The prisoners' rules of the road gave each a sense of control. Each POW could—and did—interpret these general guidelines differently. Individual responsibility and judgment gave them some daily command over how much abuse they took and how they chose to resist.

~ Speaking Truth to Power ~

Learning can come from success or failure. It can come down the chain of leadership or up the chain from the front lines.

A structure designed to protect a leader from the unvarnished truth can become an obstacle to listening and learning. The Hanoi Hilton leadership, in contrast, insisted on open communication. In addition to relaying messages, the communications network facilitated dialogue up and down the chain of command, including questions, debates, and disagreements. Chuck Boyd believes the ability to speak truth to power is critical.

Long after his years in the Hanoi Hilton, when Boyd was a colonel, he had occasion to disagree openly with a senior officer who also happened to be his boss. Perhaps his experience in Vietnam gave him the confidence to stand up for his convictions because he had stood up for them then. Boyd's general was proposing a major initiative, one that would affect the way an Air Force command was jointly organized with the other services. Boyd thought the proposal had potentially adverse political consequences for the Air Force and no operational benefit. To his mind, it was just a shaky idea, but the general was looking for Boyd's endorsement in front of the staff.

The general was a strong, type-A personality accustomed to getting his way, and he made it clear what he wanted and expected in this instance. Boyd paused briefly, turned to the numerous staff present, and said, "Clear the room." Everyone quietly filed out of the room. "Then it was just me and the three-star, and I said, 'Sir, this is a bad idea, I don't think it will work, and when it doesn't, it's going to come back in our lap in an embarrassing way. I know you have your nose out of joint right now, so if you wish, you can order me to prepare the staff work and I'll do it, but only with the understanding that I think it's simply wrong.'"

Later Boyd recalled, "He left the room mad as hell at me, but determined to push the initiative anyway." The political backlash came, as Boyd predicted, and the whole episode ended badly, an embarrassment for the Air Force.

But that's not the end of the story. The following year the same three-star general recommended Boyd for promotion to brigadier general, and several years later, as a four-star, he specifically asked for Boyd to serve in his Major Air Command. The two men are fast friends today.

"In the autumn of your years, you will reflect back on decisions that you have made, and how you've behaved, and you will be ashamed for those opportunities you had to stand up and didn't," said Boyd. "You'll feel good about yourself when you took the risks but did the right thing, no matter what the consequences."[1]

---

[1] Charles G. Boyd, interview by the authors, May 3, 2011.

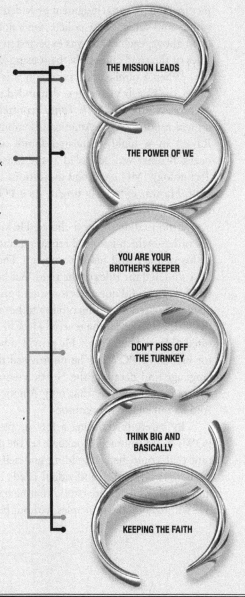

FIGURE 5.1 ~ Speaking Truth to Power

Being allowed to speak truth to power flattens the hierarchical structure of the group, placing value on the followers and their frontline observations and keeping their energies focused on the mission.

Being allowed to speak truth to power encourages mission focus. Facts and results become more important than rank and power.

Being allowed to speak truth to power encourages team members to strive for effectiveness and efficiency. Learning what works and getting results trump rank and personalities. The openness it nurtures encourages free-flowing ideas and brainstorming.

THE MISSION LEADS

THE POWER OF WE

YOU ARE YOUR BROTHER'S KEEPER

DON'T PISS OFF THE TURNKEY

THINK BIG AND BASICALLY

KEEPING THE FAITH

Each of these rules contained two critical elements—cultural expectations and room for personal judgment. Cultural expectations gave the POWs a sense of their role in the bigger picture, and personal judgment provided them personal responsibility and value. These policies were not merely handed down from above; each POW was expected to take ownership of the rules of the road and apply them using his own judgment.

When a public address system was installed in the POW camp, the North Vietnamese demanded that Alan Brudno read excerpts from *New York Times* reporter Harrison Salisbury's critical reports of the American bombing of North Vietnam. Raised in a highly educated family of doctors and engineers, Brudno was schooled at the Massachusetts Institute of Technology (MIT) and had aspirations of becoming an astronaut. He was extremely bright. As a POW, he also proved to be extremely clever.

Brudno didn't have a choice. He knew he couldn't avoid the order—which involved repeating statements highly critical of his country and his government. Those statements would have violated the rules of the road. But he also knew that most of his captors did not possess a sound grasp of the English language. He used that vulnerability to his advantage. Every time the script referenced the revered Ho Chi Minh, Brudno substituted "Horse Shit Minh." He provided hours of entertainment for his fellow POWs as he improvised the script, altering the language and derailing the North Vietnamese's brainwashing efforts in a slight way that only Americans could appreciate. And he outsmarted his captors.

By carefully choosing a few simple principles that most POWs could embrace, Stockdale set the ground rules for a culture that could be self-guiding and self-perpetuating. He set goals that both filled individual needs and served the group mission. Stockdale understood that he had to rely on others to live willingly by the principles without being micromanaged.

LEADERSHIP: MORE INSPIRATION THAN DICTATION

Because of the harsh reality of the prison environment, this hands-off approach was a necessity. Stockdale knew he had to inspire, not dictate. Humility in leadership was not an option, it was a requirement. Personal ownership and responsibility became the cultural norm for the organization, and improvisation followed. An empowered, learning, and agile culture resulted. One of the most frequent management styles cited by repatriates in their later professional lives is precisely the style Stockdale modeled. As former POW Ed Mechenbier says, "Leadership is 98 percent about empowerment, and about two percent of the time about presenting yourself as being imperial, as saying, 'Hey, I am in charge here.'"[7]

Stockdale laid down instructions that were firm enough to guide but flexible enough to allow for innovation. It was important that he keep his expectations for the team short, simple, and balanced between the individual's needs and interests and the group's mission. Any organization that articulates simple, clear, balanced expectations has started building a culture in which individuals can support solidarity and in which personal desires can take a backseat to the common mission and common good.

FIGURE 5.2 ~ Think Big and Basically

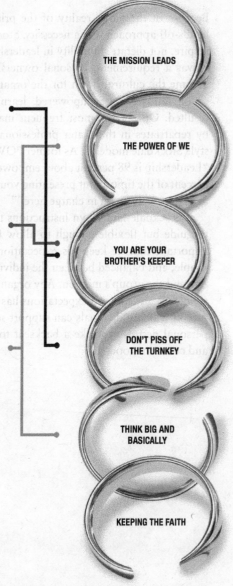

The POW leadership expected personal improvisation, learning, and communication about lessons learned among the prisoners. Because the rules of the road were so general, each person was expected to improvise, learn, and share what he learned. The knowledge and lessons learned spread from cell to cell as a manifestation of the POW culture of personal responsibility and empowerment.

The Hanoi Hilton POWs' high-performance culture balanced the good of the group with the needs of the individual. The collective mission was always paramount, but daily decisions on how they accomplished the mission were usually entrusted to each individual.

Their culture was based on a few simple rules of the road. These rules emphasized the group mission, but required personal judgment, took into account individual ability, and emphasized the importance of personal choice and responsibility. Many of the rules provided a sense of group expectation that defined where each individual fit into the bigger picture. They also defined personal values—that is, the responsibility and authority each individual was expected to shoulder.

THE MISSION LEADS

THE POWER OF WE

YOU ARE YOUR BROTHER'S KEEPER

DON'T PISS OFF THE TURNKEY

THINK BIG AND BASICALLY

KEEPING THE FAITH

CHAPTER 6

No Excuses:
The Foundation of a Viral Culture

66 "There were times I would hear him going through interrogation over the wall. This Vietnamese colonel was over all the camps. Stockdale treated him like the colonel worked for him. It was the closest I ever saw a Vietnamese in the camp come to being cowed. The situation called for *leadership by example* [italics added]. Stockdale knew it."[1]

Paul Galanti was twenty-six years old when he was shot down and sent to the Hanoi Hilton. James Stockdale was twenty years his senior. And Galanti was in awe. Not only was Stockdale enduring unimaginable physical torture, but he was successfully manipulating the colonel at his own game. "Here was this forty-six-year-old geezer going through the same stuff I was facing," recalls Galanti. But Stockdale was somehow turning the tables on the interrogations and taking control of the situation. "There was no way I was going to back off, knowing what he was doing."[2]

A CULTURE OF NO EXCUSES

How did Stockdale do it? Once again, the clues lie in his reliance on ancient philosophy: "Epictetus emphasizes time and again that a man who lays off the causes of his actions to third parties or forces is not leveling with himself. He must live with his own judgments if he is to be honest with himself. You've got to get it *straight*! *You* are in charge of *you*."[3]

Twenty years after the prisoners' release, Stockdale was still talking about the importance of taking responsibility for what you can control and letting go of what you can't. He wrote, "The only good things of *absolute value* are those that lie within your control. They are relatively few: things like thought, impulse, our opinions, our desires, our aversions, what we conceive of, what we choose, and so on. Who is the invincible man? *He who cannot be dismayed by any happenings beyond his control* [italics added]."[4]

The POW culture did not allow for excuses. Prisoners were expected to choose how they responded to what was happening around them, and they were expected to take responsibility for their choice. They were expected to admit failure quickly, and they were expected to learn from their failures. They were expected to forgive their own failure and the failure of others. They were expected to bounce back—to get back up and keep moving toward the collective goal.

YOU CAN ALWAYS CONTROL YOU

Some of today's military mental health experts work with a similar concept in acceptance and commitment therapy (ACT), a psychological intervention tool that advocates recognizing and accepting symptoms, choosing a proactive approach to the problem based on values, and acting on that approach. Proponents say ACT can be an effective tool for coping with trauma.

Army colonel Dave Benedek, a forensic psychiatrist and associate director at the Center for the Study of Traumatic Stress at the Uniformed Services University of the Health Sciences in Bethesda, Maryland, is working with many young veterans who have recently returned from Iraq and Afghanistan. These veterans are facing major readjustment issues, and some are battling PTSD. Benedek uses ACT as a means to give these veterans some coping tools.

"ACT helps people focus on their values, and if not embrace their symptoms, recognize that they can experience symptoms without it necessarily negatively affecting their lives," says Colonel Benedek. "Despite the fact that I have crappy sleep sometimes, I can still be loyal. I can still be honest. These are the things that are important to me, and despite whatever's going on, I can continue my life according to my values. It's accepting some things that we can't do anything about, and committing to life according to one's values."[5]

At a personal level, veterans undergoing ACT focus on being true to what they want to be while not wasting energy on what they cannot change. ACT infuses the therapeutic process with a sense of personal obligation. Galanti was motivated to take personal responsibility for the POWs' mission, Return with Honor. He was inspired by Stockdale's behavior during interrogation, even without supplemental face-to-face meetings, lengthy memos, or group strategy retreats.

Holding similar values, facing a common adversary, and deeply motivated by their shared goal of returning home, most POWs were determined to defeat their captors. In order to defeat them, they needed to resist them, and in order to resist them, they needed to control their own behavior and their attitudes. These were the only things they could control.

Modeling this behavior was hard. But, with leaders like Stockdale providing an example, the motivation to perform well was high. To keep spirits up, the prisoners needed a means to spread that inspiration and motivation throughout the organization.

SETTING EXPECTATIONS FOR PERSONAL RESPONSIBILITY

Schooled in the traditions of the Stoics, Stockdale understood the process necessary to enroot that individual sense of responsibility in a hostile environment. He labeled those who chose to join the process citizens, not followers. According to Stockdale,

This required that we first build a culture. And because most of us were in solitary confinement, this culture had to spread by faint but rhythmic tapping signals picked up by ears pressed to the bottom of drinking cups, open ends strategically placed at listening posts along prison walls. We came to live by those taps and responses, transmitting orders, encouragement, and solidarity in paragraph after paragraph. Without tools or paper and pencil, nothing but brains, stealth, knuckles, and drinking-cup listening devices, our society took root and grew—a society of our own making with our own laws, customs, traditions, heroes, folklore, and citizens.[6]

A steady drumbeat, the communications network was a reminder of the mission and the practices necessary to achieve it. It was the lifeblood of the fragile POW culture. Without it, the cultural norms that Stockdale established would not have permeated the organization.

The responsibility of each citizen was understood by all: "Each citizen of the cell block of Hoa Lo prison in Hanoi grew to proceed from the assumption that his society's fate was *his fate* and that he was therefore responsible for its fate and its honor. *Death before dishonor. Unity over self.* We came to live by phrases like these [italics added]."[7]

This early initiation—exposure to the culture and its expectations for each and every POW—was critical. The sooner the prisoners could reach out to a new shoot-down, the better the chances of getting him to embrace the culture and become an active citizen in the resistance effort. They all endured the initiation "crucible," and it ensured that their drive to share information was unstoppable.

BEATING THE ODDS

The results obtained by the Hanoi Hilton prisoner culture stand in stark contrast to what the POW populations from other wars experienced and achieved. POW stories from the Korean War and World War II often reflected what game theorists call the "prisoner's dilemma," a term first coined more than fifty years ago to describe how the raw self-interest of an individual often overrides the cooperation that would produce the best outcome for a group.

James Clavell's 1960s' best seller *King Rat* fictionalizes the author's real-life experiences in a World War II POW camp, in which the general rule was "every man for himself." In this story, an American Army corporal reigns over a vast population of Allied POWs who surrendered the naval base in Singapore and were held captive by the Japanese in the notorious and forbidding Changi prison camp, where more than 30,000 men were held from 1942 until liberation in 1945. Nicknamed "the King," this powerful but corrupt soldier took advantage of the prisoner's quandry and maximized it for his own personal gain—more food, better living conditions, money, and brutal control over other POWs.

The prisoners held in this camp were not confined to cells but lived in a village-like community surrounded by a wall. The men could move about freely inside a lightly guarded perimeter, but they were on an island an ocean away from home. Where could they go?

Food and medical supplies were scarce. Most of the POWs suffered from malnutrition and debilitating ailments, such as dysentery and beriberi, but not the King:

> The whole of Changi hated the King. They hated him for his muscular body, the clear glow in his blue eyes. In this twilight world of the half alive there were no fat or well-built or round or smooth or fair-built or thick-built men. There were only faces dominated by eyes and set on bodies that were skin over sinews over bones. No differences between them but age and face and height. And in all this world, only the King ate like a man, smoked like a man, slept like a man, dreamed like a man and looked like a man.[8]

The King coerced and stole money, food, and supplies from his captors and fellow prisoners, playing one against the other. While most of the POWs at Changi survived by teaming up in small units to forage, scavenge, and hoard food and supplies, the King operated independently and trusted no one. He was aware that the POWs envied him, and it amused him. He was proud of his accomplishments and the corrupt fiefdom he had created. Wrote Clavell, "Through cunning he had created a world. He surveyed his world and was well satisfied."[9]

As the King saw it, he was just doing what he had to do to survive. In his own mind, "The world was a jungle, and the strong survived and the weak should die. It was you or the other guy. That's right. There is no other way."[10]

How did this happen? How did a large group of well-trained, combat-seasoned military men—from the United States, Australia, the United Kingdom, and Canada—in captivity end up pitting one against another, resorting to the basest of instincts, and showing a lack of camaraderie that would have been anathema in a fighting unit?

In 2011 Dr. Hamish Ion, a professor of history at the Royal Military College of Canada, published a study of senior military officers in the Changi camp titled "Brass Hats behind Bamboo Palisades: Senior Officer POWs in Singapore, Taiwan, and Manchukuo, 1942–45." The study explained how the stress of captivity can bring out different personality traits. In a simple comparison of the senior officers in Changi and the POWs in the Hanoi Hilton, a student of history might not find much difference. But, Ion dug a bit deeper by examining the personal writings of two British officers—Brigadier Hubert Francis "Hoodie" Lucas and Brigadier Bernard Stanley Challen—and other papers held at the Imperial War Museum in London. In these two men's writings, he found two salient characteristics: (1) no complete uniformity of response to imprisonment among the senior officers and (2) a defensive need by these senior officers to restore their reputations, which had been damaged in the military defeat that led to their incarceration.

In other words, these POWs blamed their senior officers for their surrender and incarceration. Ion wrote, "[In order to] salvage their own reputations, they would have to savage those with whom they shared captivity."[11] The internal dissent and lack of unity among the POW leaders at Changi were established at the outset of captivity and only worsened over the duration of the incarceration. And the individual prisoners took no personal responsibility for the group—only for themselves.

THOSE WHO LEAD HOLD ONE ADDITIONAL RESPONSIBILITY

Stockdale understood that the cultural pendulum could have gone the other way in the Hanoi Hilton. He wrote, "A sense of selfless unity, a nobility of that spirit that seemed to run counter to conventional views on survival instinct grew up among us. It became commonplace for one man to risk greatly to save another. I don't believe it *always* happens that way. There are stories of those in crisis who savagely turn against each other— all against all. Whether the best or worst in men emerges as they face crises together swings on the quality of leadership available to them."[12]

It is surprising that a captive military culture, totally isolated from the outside world, hobbled with a primitive communication method, still managed to create a more flexible and agile organization—a better learning organization—than modern companies can build using the latest technology, consultants, and nearly limitless access to information. For many of the POWs, the prisoner culture forged such powerful bonds over time that it rewarded them with a sense of self, accomplishment, and fulfillment, even in the face of uncommon deprivation and hardship.

FIGURE 6.1 ~ No Excuses

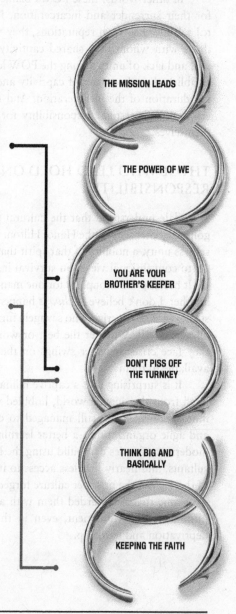

The POW leaders shaped the culture by modeling commitment to the group mission. Sacrificial actions by leaders and inclusive communication from the moment a prisoner entered the prison told the POWs that the group "had their back." It also clearly told them that they were expected to behave in the same manner. This reciprocal commitment—flowing from the group to the individual and from the individual to the group—proved to be critical to overcoming the human tendency toward an "every prisoner for himself" culture.

The high-performance POW culture was based on taking responsibility for the one thing you can always control: yourself. As younger POWs such as Paul Galanti watched middle-aged veteran James Stockdale willingly walk into the torture cell time after time, they learned that they did have choices, and that insight gave them an unexpected freedom. Their ability to understand that the most important thing in their current circumstances was always under their control proved to be critical to their long-term resilience and mission success.

THE MISSION LEADS

THE POWER OF WE

YOU ARE YOUR BROTHER'S KEEPER

DON'T PISS OFF THE TURNKEY

THINK BIG AND BASICALLY

KEEPING THE FAITH

CHAPTER 7

Don't Piss Off the Turnkey: Focusing on What You Can Control

"There was absolutely no reason to piss off a turn-key," Charlie Zuhoski says. The low-level camp guard who was responsible for bringing the POWs their meals and letting them out of their cells for short periods of time to bathe and empty their toilet buckets was not worth the aggravation. "They had little authority. They just did what they were told. But if you pissed one of them off, you could spend the next twenty hours without food or water in a cell that was 120 degrees. But some guys would still lose their cool and take their frustration out on the turnkey."[1]

Staying focused on the group mission required individual discipline and focus, and not everybody in the Hanoi Hilton acted like a professional all the time. Not everybody focused his energy on what was important. Not everybody channeled his resources into winning. But that was the collective goal: choose your battles carefully.

STOCKDALE'S HEDGEHOG: "ALL IN" COMMITMENT

James Stockdale held up the hedgehog as a model for leaders who wanted to win in battle. In a 1991 lecture he gave at the U.S. Naval Academy, he paraphrased an ancient Greek poet: "The clever fox knows many things, but the hedgehog knows one big thing. . . . And the one big thing these hedgehogs know is, 'Blast out; go for the jugular, never hesitate to lay down your life for your friends.'"[2] For Stockdale and the POWs, protecting their fellow POWs was a battle worth fighting.

"HE WAS PROTECTING ME"

One hot summer night in 1967, in the part of the prison the POWs called Thunderbird, Stockdale and Sam Johnson were making repeated attempts to communicate with a group of new guys, recent shoot-downs who were most likely recovering from their ejection injuries and overwhelmed by their new circumstances. As Johnson described it, "They were scared, for good reason. We wanted to talk to them and make them know that there were other Americans around."[3]

This was a more challenging and odious task than Johnson casually described because it required "clearing for the guards." The tap code was the POWs' lifeblood, but the punishment for communicating with each other—in any way—was harsh. So harsh, in fact, that whenever possible, the POWs assigned at least one man to the task of clearing for the guards, that is, alerting the POWs to the guards' impending approach. This sometimes required lying on the filthy prison cell floor, which was often covered in human excrement and insects, and peering through the crack under the prison door, looking for changes in the light that would signal someone was walking by. Or it would entail balancing on a toilet bucket—again a precarious task, as the buckets usually contained waste—to look over the top of the cell door for shadows moving along the hallway, indicating an approaching guard. When someone was detected, the one "clearing" would urgently signal in any way he could: shouting, coughing, bumping against the wall. In most instances, the POWs had only a few seconds to cease their communication efforts and feign innocence.

"Stockdale had a broken leg, of course, and I had a busted arm and the bunks were, you know, about that high and concrete," Johnson explained, holding his hand up to his knees. Johnson is a tall man and probably needed about an extra three feet to be able to peer out a high window. "Jim would get on the floor and 'clear,' and I'd get up on the concrete bunk and talk to [a new guy] down the back side out of the window. We happened to be on the back of the jail. And, you know, we would tell him essentially how the cow eats the cabbage [how the things worked in the prison system] and, that 'you're going to be all right.'"[4]

That night in 1967 they were caught. According to Johnson,

I was talking down the back, and the guard and an officer came charging down the hall. And Jim was under the door, of course, and I was on the bunk, and he barely got up before the door opened. The guys didn't give us much warning on them coming, and I got off the bunk and I'm standing there and the door pops open and here's this little North Vietnamese guy wearing Air Force second lieutenant bars. Turns out he was a camp commander. He wasn't a lieutenant—he was masquerading as one. Jim hauled off and decked him right there. Just knocked him down. And, I thought, "Oh my God, we're in deep serious now." And we were.[5]

The ramifications were immediate and harsh. The Vietnamese punished both men. Johnson was sequestered in a little room by himself. His captors boarded up the windows and put him in leg stocks for seventy-two days.

Why did Stockdale intentionally assault the camp commander by punching him in the face? Was he caught up in a fit of anger, or was there some method to his madness? Johnson was deliberate in his response to these questions: "Frankly, I think he was protecting me. . . . And, you know, that's a characteristic of leadership, too."[6]

Both Johnson and Stockdale were punished for their actions that day, but Stockdale took the brunt of the force. He had chosen his battle carefully and sacrificed himself for

Johnson—and for the mission—that day. Bringing the new guys into the fold, telling them the mission, credo, and rules of the road, teaching them how to communicate and stay connected with each other, and reassuring them that the leadership would protect them—all this was worth the risk of being caught. And, when the punishment came, Stockdale was willing to take the brunt of it. Stockdale couldn't control much that day, but he could control who received the lion's share of the punishment for communicating with the other prisoners.

ONE FREEDOM YOU ALWAYS HAVE: TO CHOOSE YOUR RESPONSE

A sense of efficacy—however meager—was critical to the POWs' mental health. Once again the recurring theme of "no excuses" surfaces: the prisoners responded to their bleak existence without most basic human rights by focusing on what they could control. In an environment characterized by few freedoms, few choices, and little power, Stockdale's actions were a type of power play—the strongest he could muster.

In *Man's Search for Meaning*, Dr. Viktor Frankl reminds readers of one sense of efficacy that can never be taken away, even when forces beyond your control take away everything else you possess: your freedom to choose how you will respond to a situation. Every day Stockdale and many of the POWs consciously chose freedom with regard to their attitudes, one of the few aspects of their lives they could control. They chose not to be victims. Indeed, their daily acts of resistance, their continuous attempts to stay connected with each other, and their adherence to the mission—Return with Honor—boosted their confidence and took the word "victim" right out of their individual and collective vocabulary. "Was I a victim? Not when I became fully engaged, got into the life of unity with comrades, helping others and being encouraged by them. So many times, I would find myself whispering to myself after an exhilarating wall tap message exchange: I am right where I belong; I am right where I was meant to be," wrote Stockdale.[7]

Frankl—and Stockdale's Stoic philosophy—emphasize that when you have no other freedom, the choice over how you will respond can be a lifeline. That solitary choice—or sense of control—is a powerful antidote to helplessness and despair, one that scientists frequently cite as a major contributor to mental health and an individual's personal hardiness.

CHOOSING TO STAY BATTLE FIT

It was tough for individual prisoners to sustain their sense of personal control. Stripped of most basic human rights, the POWs forced themselves to frame their response to their condition as a "choice." Instinctively, they turned to mental and physical exercises as a remedy—as both a healthy distraction and a source of strength building. Physical and mental exercise allowed them to preserve their energy for the battles worth fighting. They memorized names of fellow POWs (in the event they had a chance to relay information to the outside world), designed houses in their heads, replayed sporting events in which they had participated, or learned foreign languages from fellow POWs through the tap code.

Everett Alvarez admits that it took him a while to effectively use his mind to combat the boredom, frustration, sadness, and uncertainty that faced him on a daily basis while in captivity. At first, he says, he resisted crying. "I was brought up, as most American boys, to believe that men don't cry." But, he now knows that his crying spells were actually cathartic: "They seemed to have the effect of cleansing my mind so that I could concentrate on things I could do instead of things I couldn't." And that's when he began work on his own version of "reframing."[8]

He describes the intense mental clarity he experienced when all the outside stimuli of normal life were taken away.

He quickly realized that the only thing he had control over in captivity was his mind, so he put it to use. He invented rituals similar to prayer that sharpened his memory and helped him focus on productive tasks. In addition to daily physical exercise,

> I also started reliving events in my life during a period I set aside for this exercise in the later afternoon. I would reconstruct a day with all of its happenings minute-by-minute. During these sessions I tried to remember all the names of individuals associated with particular events, usually from school or college years. It was quite a challenge. I would summon up a group or class picture and then match names. I did pretty well, as I learned when I came home. I would bump into people I hadn't seen since childhood and surprise them by asking about brother "Jim" or sister "Mary" or whether their parents still lived on Sycamore Street. "How can you remember that?," they'd ask. Easy. Working at it saved my life.[9]

Physical exercise—even in extremely confined spaces— was also a means of control, and it helped ward off the deterioration of the body. "By Christmas of 1968 our physical condition had deteriorated badly and I'm sure our individual mental conditions were at the same low level," wrote Jim Mulligan in his autobiography *The Hanoi Commitment.*

> Each day I maintained a continuous, vigorous exercise program conducted in the 4 x 4 ½ area available. I ran in place, did knee bends, arm stretches and hip twists. My broken shoulder and torn muscles gradually healed to a point where I could do a few mild, half-hearted pushups. . . . I had good wind from running in place and I felt I could make it to the 17th parallel if I could get out. My feet were toughened from calluses built up from running in place on the

concrete floor. I started each day by running at least 2,000 counts on my left foot at as rapid a pace as I could maintain.[10]

CHOOSING TO GIVE MEANING TO LOST TIME

In his book *Bouncing Back*, author Geoffrey Norman describes mental and physical exercise as providing a release and giving purpose to the POWs' idle time.[11] But exercise was also a way of exerting control over their situation—most notably when they were physically separated from each other and forced to endure solitary confinement. In other words, when in solitary confinement, the prisoners focused their energy on turning the isolation to their advantage. As a result, the time they spent in prison was not lost; rather, it was redeemed and given meaning.

By 1970 the interrogations, isolation, and restrictions had decreased significantly. The prisoners were placed in larger group cells with forty or more men, and they were allowed to go outside, exercise, and socialize on a regular basis. They reveled in these newfound freedoms and took advantage of them as well. Mulligan wrote, "The large cells became beehives of non-stop activity: high-stake poker games, chess and bridge tournaments, walkers getting their exercise while dodging men doing handstands or practicing golf swings, scribblers working on correspondence or communications notes. Every cell had its raconteurs and resident experts. Swede Larson expounded for hours on the science of raising chickens for profit . . . [and] Mike Brazelton was one of several talented 'movie tellers.'"[12]

And the academics? According to Rochester and Kiley, "Informal study groups . . . evolved into a full-fledged 'university.' . . . An eclectic 'curriculum' included history, political science, mathematics, literature, at least four foreign languages (Spanish, French, German and Russian), and numerous 'electives' ranging from music and art appreciation to skiing, beekeeping, and diesel maintenance."[13]

CHOOSING TO MANAGE YOUR ENERGY

While most of the POWs would probably describe their efforts at exercise as a method of strengthening their bodies and minds, scientists today might call this tactic "energy management." Tony Schwartz is the president and founder of the Energy Project in New York City, which has coached thousands of business leaders and managers of large organizations. To a person, these executives describe the 24-7 work cycle as one that requires constant feeding and attention. But it is within the capacity of individual employees to "recognize the costs of energy-depleting behaviors and then take responsibility for changing them, regardless of the circumstances they're facing. . . . Energy can be systematically expanded and regularly renewed by establishing specific rituals—behaviors that are intentionally practiced and precisely scheduled, with the goal of making them unconscious and automatic as quickly as possible."[14]

What the POWs had discovered on their own was that their physical and mental routines—or rituals—enabled them to better manage their energy levels. Managing their time was not a high priority, as they had endless amounts of it. Managing their well-being and exerting some control over their condition were.

"We have far more control over our energy than we ordinarily realize. The number of hours in a day is fixed, but the quantity and quality of energy available to us is not," write Jim Loehr and Schwartz, coauthors of *The Power of Full Engagement.* Loehr and Schwartz say that the skillful management of energy is what produces the most productive, healthy, and happy lives. The term "full engagement" refers to being "physically energized, emotionally connected, mentally focused and spiritually aligned with a purpose beyond our immediate self-interest."[15]

CHOOSING WHAT WORKS FOR YOU:
ONE SIZE DOES NOT FIT ALL

A person's energy "tanks" are depleted at different rates. The key is to find a way to replenish those tanks, or bounce back. West Point's Dr. Zinsser, the sports psychologist at the CEP, stresses the importance of savoring small pleasures and fleeting moments. "It's the ability to draw strength, solace, something positive from the very tiniest opportunity," says Zinsser. "If you give me a blade of grass, I'm really going to appreciate it."[16]

POW Mike Christian's energy was derived from an act of resistance. John McCain told a story about Christian in a speech at the 1988 Republican National Convention:

> Mike came from a small town near Selma, Alabama. He didn't wear a pair of shoes until he was thirteen years old. At seventeen, he enlisted in the U.S. Navy. He later earned a commission by going to Officer Training School. Then he became a Naval Flight Officer and was shot down and captured in 1967. The Vietnamese allowed some prisoners to receive packages from home. In some of these packages were handkerchiefs, scarves and other items of clothing. Mike got himself a bamboo needle. Over a period of a couple of months, he created an American flag and sewed it on the inside of his shirt.[17]

In a daily ritual the POWs performed as a group prior to eating their meager food ration of a bowl of soup, McCain explained, he, Christian, and the others in their cell would hang Mike's shirt on the wall and say the Pledge of Allegiance together. Both the sewing exercise and the recitation of the pledge were forbidden by camp rules, and once again, the POWs knew the consequences of getting caught. Sure enough, they eventually were. According to McCain,

> One day the Vietnamese searched our cell, as they did periodically, and discovered Mike's shirt with the

flag sewn inside, and removed it. That evening they returned, opened the door of the cell, and for the benefit of all of us, beat Mike Christian severely for the next couple of hours. Then, they opened the door of the cell and threw him in. We cleaned him up as well as we could.

The cell in which we lived had a concrete slab in the middle on which we slept. Four naked light bulbs hung in each corner of the room. As I said, we tried to clean up Mike as well as we could. After the excitement died down, I looked in the corner of the room, and sitting there beneath that dim light bulb with a piece of red cloth, another shirt and his bamboo needle, was my friend, Mike Christian. He was sitting there with his eyes almost shut from the beating he had received, making another American flag.[18]

Mike Christian had found his own antidote to powerlessness.

FIGURE 7.1 ~ Don't Piss Off the Turnkey

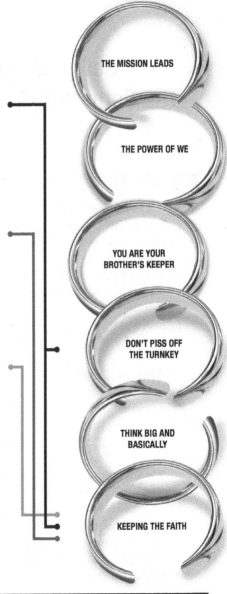

The POWs seized every opportunity for victory. Every time a message was tapped out on a cell wall, the prisoners had a small success to celebrate. Every time they could turn their assigned task of working in the courtyard—either sweeping or coughing to communicate with the same tap code matrix—they won a small but psychologically important victory.

The Hanoi Hilton POW culture stressed attending to the issues you could control and letting go of those that you could not control. Although the POWs did not always agree on what could be controlled, they learned to focus most of their resources on their own personal decisions, responses, and actions. Remaining rationally focused on what could be controlled and tuning out the uncontrollable proved critical to their emotional well-being and mission success.

The POWs who understood that their battle was mostly mental appear to be the ones who handled their environment most successfully. The Vietnamese captors could and did physically control the POWs, and so the six inches between the prisoners' ears became the real battleground. Mental resolve proved to be the key to the POWs' ultimate victory.

THE MISSION LEADS

THE POWER OF WE

YOU ARE YOUR BROTHER'S KEEPER

DON'T PISS OFF THE TURNKEY

THINK BIG AND BASICALLY

KEEPING THE FAITH

CHAPTER 8

Get on the Wall:
The Catharsis of Confession

R obbie Risner remembers it as a bad one:

On this particular day they were making someone scream pretty loud. Later they brought him over to Heartbreak, threw him in a cell, locked the door, and went away. As soon as we were sure it was safe, we began to try to talk to whoever it was they had been working on. When we asked him if he had been injured, he told us that he had broken his thigh when he bailed out.

I asked, "Was that you we heard scream a while ago?"

There was a pause, and then kind of quietly he said, "Yes."

Someone said, "What did they do to you? Were they torturing you?"

He replied, "No, they were just twisting my broken leg when I wouldn't talk!"

He felt crushed because he had talked; he figured now he was a traitor. We all knew the mental anguish he was going through because most of us had been there ourselves. One survival technique we developed, though, was to try to be absolutely honest about what we had "confessed." After we were tortured, we would tell the others every bit of information we had given. If we had said something, for example, about the communications system, it was absolutely imperative that the word was put out so we could be prepared for whatever might come.

Sometimes it really hurt to be honest, but the longer we were there, the more we appreciated it because it helped everybody.[1]

~ Get Real: Leaning into Your Fears ~

Although they are not conformists and have differing personalities, the POWs who endured the Hanoi Hilton experience all exude quiet confidence and a noticeable certainty of purpose. However, most of them are also quick to stress that they have feet of clay. Their considerable accomplishments are tempered by their awareness of their own limitations. They discovered these limitations through a severe test of their individual breaking points. These limitations were hard earned. As Lee Ellis puts it, they learned to "lean into their fears."

"When I say 'lean into the fear,' it really comes down to your inner confidence," says Ellis. "And I have the confidence today to do most anything that I need to do, to confront anybody or to be humble and to be humbled. I can cry if I need to cry. Or I can be as tough as nails. I'm not perfect, but I'm a lot tougher guy [than I used to be]."

Ellis says watching men who successfully withstood torture taught him how to handle it—how to lean into his fear. He adds, "People who had competed in individual sports were tougher going into torture than people who hadn't. When you're a wrestler or a swimmer or a tennis player and you've had to go to battle one-on-one, you're much better equipped than somebody who's only played team sports, to go into one-on-one with an interrogator because you have a different level of confidence of fighting alone. The guys who were the toughest were the wrestlers and tennis players and the runners."[1]

Thinking through the fears that restrain you from trying to accomplish your dreams, the fears that keep you from risking more, the fears that cause you to choke at critical moments, the fears of failing that keep you from succeeding—that is leaning into your fear. The POWs had the time and the impetus to overcome fears that would hold others back. This motivation made them high-performing.

(continued)

In the U.S. military's effort to help veterans from the conflicts in Iraq and Afghanistan to confront their PTSD, one tool that is showing promise is virtual-reality therapy. Using technology developed for video games, researchers have created software that simulates combat scenarios complete with the sounds and smells of battle. The software forces veterans to face their fears again and again. The theory is that facing those fears—instead of avoiding them—will speed up recovery. The veterans are leaning into their fear using video-game technology.

Leaning into your fears involves getting hit, getting hurt, and failing. The Hanoi Hilton POWs expected to be bruised and beaten down. They knew they would face pain and torture, and they understood there would be failures. They learned to admit their own fears and weaknesses. They learned to accept their own humanness and limitations, as well as the humanness and limitations of others on their team.

They learned to lean into their fears and found that they could withstand more than they thought. In facing their fears, they overcame them.

---

[1] Lee Ellis, interview by the authors, September 19, 2011.

PROVIDING SAFETY: CELLS AS CONFESSIONALS

The honesty initially hurt, but confessing was ultimately cathartic. The prisoners were required to spill their guts to their teammates after an interrogation session. Stockdale's imperative to new shoot-downs was simple: "Get on the wall." It was the mantra repeated by the POWs to their friends after particularly tough interrogations or when one sensed that a fellow POW was depressed or suffering. "Get on the wall" meant "Talk to me. Don't suffer alone. If you broke under the pressure, get over it." The wall allowed both intimacy and a bit of anonymity. It aided individuals in revealing their deepest fears and darkest secrets, but this sharing was often conducted with strangers, as many of the POWs had never laid eyes on each other.

The leaders of the POW organization knew that even the most strident resister among them had physical and mental breaking points. Resisting beyond those individual limits risked long-term physical injury or death with no valuable return for the effort; they would still be POWs with no idea when they would be released. So, each man used whatever resistance tactics worked best for him until he could resist no more physically or mentally. And then he got on the wall to recover and prepare for the next interrogation session—which he knew would come sooner or later.

Beyond helping others and serving the team mission, Stockdale knew the moments spent kneeling on the floor of the cell tapping out what information you had given up in the pain of torture had a deeper benefit. It was a confessional.

HONESTY BREEDS TRUST; TRUST BREEDS UNITY

"Getting on the wall" meant finding that safe place to talk about the traumatic incident just experienced; it was the therapy and the forgiveness all at once. And it allowed the POWs to fail without being a failure. Indeed, the organization and the leaders fostered a culture in which risk taking and innovation in the face of such trauma were rewarded. The larger organization turned individual failures into a strategy for long-term success in the collective resistance effort.

A decade after the prisoners' return home, Stockdale explained the progression in one sentence: "Any American who from his solitary cell was caught communicating with another American, by wall tap, by whisper, you name it, was put back in the meat grinder to go from torture to submission to confession to apology to atonement."[2]

ADMITTING FAILURE QUICKLY

Reliving the experience in the immediate aftermath had another effect. It sped up the prisoners' recovery from traumatic incidents.

Al Stafford was piloting his A-4 over North Vietnam when it was blown out of the air by a surface-to-air missile. He was captured and subjected to a series of interrogation sessions, during which his untreated injuries made the torture even more excruciating. Desperate not to give up valuable intelligence, he resisted his interrogators' initial softball questions: name, rank, serial number, the name of his ship. Of the incident author Geoffrey Norman wrote, "Finally, after an hour or so, they left, and for a few moments Stafford felt a surge of hope, something close to elation. *That's it. I've done it. I've won. I didn't give them anything they didn't obviously have, and now they're through with me.* For a while he was even able to ignore the pain in his arms and chest."[3]

But his captors were just getting warmed up. They came back a few hours later to ask him more questions: about future targets his squadron was planning to hit, the altitude at which he was flying, bombing tactics. As the questions became more detailed and the intelligence value higher, the torture tactics became more vicious. Instead of hitting and kicking him, they employed the rope trick. As the interrogators pulled on one end of the rope, it forced Stafford's arms higher and higher above his head, essentially pulling his arms out of their sockets. Norman continued, "He was passing out, now, then coming to and blacking out again. Without actually deciding to, he started answering the questions, whether he knew the answer or not, whether there was an answer or no. . . . Finally, his interrogator seemed satisfied with his answers. 'You have a good attitude, Stafford,' one of the interrogators said. He gave him a small cup of water. Stafford drank it with pitiful, infantile gratitude."[4]

The shame Stafford felt at his behavior was almost more than he could bear. He had to admit to himself that he had been broken—for a cup of water. He was deeply depressed and contemplated how he might commit suicide. Taking his own life seemed to be the only way to avoid giving in to the torture again.

Then, one day about a month later, he was transferred from his solitary cell to a new cell with two roommates, Bob Sawhill and Tom Parrott. They started talking—first about their respective military careers, then about how they were shot down, and then about the torture. Norman recounted the conversation: "At last Stafford decided that he would have to say it, that he could not hide what he had done forever, and that if the others were going to ostracize him, then he would just have to get used to it. . . . 'Ah, when they asked me questions, and started working me over, I'm afraid I didn't do too well. I mean . . . I gave them a little more than just name, rank, and serial number. . . . I tried to hold out but . . . well, shit, I just couldn't. They broke me.'" The silence was deafening. Stafford was sure Sawhill and Parrott were stunned by his confession. "Finally, one of them spoke. 'You too?' he said. 'Well then, join the fucking club.'"[5] And then his new cellmates poured their hearts out with similar tales.

For the first time in many weeks, Stafford felt better. He actually experienced a restful night's sleep. He realized that he was not alone and that, although he had been broken by his captors, he was not a broken man. It all came down to perspective.

THE EFFECT OF A LISTENING CULTURE

Dick Stratton, who became a therapist after he returned from Vietnam and retired from the Navy, thinks that these confessions aided the POWs' long-term recovery and led to lower rates of PTSD. "The Navy and Marine Corps were convinced that we would all be nuts [when we returned home]," he remembers. The prisoners' wives were actually told to expect the men to be infantile, impotent, or psychotic.

> They were aghast when we came home in a semi-normal state. They didn't understand that you're there for six or seven years and after the brutality stops you either sit around and pick mattress stuffing out of your belly button or do something productive. In effect, we ended up doing in prison what I do now with Vietnam vets in group therapy. You sit there and dump out all your doubts and fears with cellmates. Sort out what you have control over and what you don't. Start making plans. We weren't smart enough to know what we

were doing but we did it. We took care of our therapy. Took care of the guilt. We were adjusted to what we had done and hadn't done. We had done our best and tough luck if somebody didn't like it.[6]

The psychological benefits of confessing painful secrets are well documented. The twentieth-century psychiatrist Theodore Reik coined the term "the compulsion to confess" and alleged that the urge to confess is normal and healthy. Indeed, keeping harmful secrets can be destructive and lead to increased stress and its related indicators (increased blood pressure, perspiration, and breathing rates and a decreased immune response).[7] Keeping secrets can also lead to addiction, a decrease in intimacy, and psychological isolation. Getting it off your chest can be both physically and psychologically therapeutic. Indeed, as most Catholics know, confession has its benefits.

~ Forgiveness: The Key to Bounce Back ~

Why did James Stockdale insist on forgiveness? Forgiveness can offer practical benefits for many types of relationships, whether between two people, two families, two departments, or two nations. It is often relegated to the sphere of faith and religion. But it is frequently overlooked as a useful and practical tool for high-performance organizations.

Stockdale's approach to forgiveness offered redemption for the individual and for others. He understood the relationship that existed between failure, personal responsibility, and continued faith in ultimate success. How do you accept failure without allowing it to dominate your attitude? How do you accept responsibility without wallowing in guilt and fear of future failure? How do you keep faith in your future success while admitting—and accepting responsibility for—current failure?

To a philosopher like Stockdale, there was clear and obvious tension between these ideas. His solution was forgiveness, exemplified by his "bounce back" mandate, which allowed the POWs a type of absolution, or clean slate, after a failure. Forgiveness resolved the tension between taking personal responsibility for current failure and striving for ultimate success. This is the practical, cultural underpinning of a learning organization.

(continued)

Learning organizations outpace competitors owing to their drive to innovate and create. With innovation and creation come false starts, mistakes, and errors in judgment. Learning organizations admit missteps, allow them, accept responsibility for them, and learn from them. In this dynamic process, learning organizations forgive their members and keep driving toward the collective goals. They also outperform organizations that fear failure, avoid personal responsibility, and fail to forgive. They are high-performing.

When the POWs were thrown back into their cell after an interrogation session, Stockdale asked one thing of them. As soon as they could physically muster the strength, they were directed to kneel on the dirty floor of their cell and tap out their failure to the POW in the cell next door. The next person going in for a "quiz" needed to know whatever information or disinformation had been given up during previous interrogation sessions. The knowledge could be useful to the interrogator's next victim, as his duty was either to continue to spin the disinformation or to distort the true information the Vietnamese had squeezed out of his fellow prisoner.

Far more important, however, was the cathartic effect of sharing information for the confessor. The neighbor who quickly tapped out "God bless you" or "I love you" as his fellow prisoner was led away for an interrogation session was the same man who was there afterward with a willing ear. He listened, forgave, and provided reassurance that no matter what transpired in the interrogation session, the confessor was still one with the group. Stockdale clearly understood the symbolism of this act. Years later he wrote, "The sting of guilt was taken out of the program by the commonsense expedient of never keeping secrets from other Americans. No matter what you said or were forced to say under torture in the privacy of the interrogation room, we routinely put out the details on our tap code network. This was a natural for tactical defense and expediency, but its fallout in terms of expiation of guilt feelings was golden. We learned that the virtues of truthfulness and straightforwardness have their own reward."[1]

---

[1] James Bond Stockdale, *Thoughts of a Philosophical Fighter Pilot* (Stanford, CA: Hoover Institution Press, 1995), 7.

THE BENEFITS OF DISCLOSURE

Dr. Richard G. Tedeschi, professor of psychology at the University of North Carolina–Charlotte, has been studying the effect of trauma for years and has identified disclosure as an aid in mitigating the effect. He is a pioneer in defining and studying posttraumatic growth (PTG). He and his colleague,

Dr. Lawrence G. Calhoun, coined the term. The PTG phenomenon is a focus of the clinical and research community that is
gaining in popularity. The concept was borrowed from earlier
research that identified personal growth in the face of significant loss or suffering.

Dr. Tedeschi and Dr. Calhoun identified a number of personal, interpersonal, and cultural factors that, if present, contribute significantly to PTG. They use the term "distal cultural
elements" to define the broad geographic areas, communities,
or social networks within which individuals interact. They
allege that few psychologists and scholars study the impact of
these "cultures," but they should: "Attending to these cultural
themes and more 'distant' sources of social influence is desir-
able to understand the possibilities for growth in the struggle
with crisis."[8] In the case of the POWs, their cultural hab-
its—ingrained by their leaders—made a big difference in their
short- and long-term health.

The first factor that Dr. Tedeschi and Dr. Calhoun identify
is "disclosure," that is, the responses of others to the disclosure
of traumatic incidents. The second factor is the degree to which
an affected person's "ruminations," or what he or she believes
about the traumatic incident, are congruent with those of the
others. In other words, if the affected person finds a sympathetic
ear or, even better, someone who has been through the same
experience and has the same internal reaction, he or she will be
more likely to adapt and heal from the experience. The third
factor is the presence of models of PTG.[9] For the POWs, the
old-timers were their role models. Men such as Everett Alvarez,
who had been in captivity since 1964 and who continued to
resist his captors for more than eight years, inspired them.

Dr. Tedeschi and Dr. Calhoun go on to allege that confession increases future resilience in individuals: "Disclosure
of stressful experiences may regulate emotion by changing the
focus of attention, increasing habituation to negative emotions,
and facilitating positive cognitive reappraisals of threats."[10]

"You know, growth is the result of this shattered world,"
Dr. Tedeschi says. "When your belief system is having a hard

time keeping up with what's happened to you, you have to really penetrate into that system and take a look at what it is that you should be believing and what makes sense given what's happened to you. So, that spurs people to some kind of change. I mean growth is change."[11]

He and Dr. Calhoun wrote, "Posttraumatic growth, then, may not necessarily be 'good' from a utilitarian perspective—the presence of PTG may not necessarily be accompanied by greater well-being and less distress. However, if the perspective is broadened, the data does seem to suggest that the presence of PTG is an indication that persons who experience it are living life in ways that, at least from their own point of view, are fuller, richer, and perhaps more meaningful."[12]

Those who experience PTG are able to jettison negative thoughts about their trauma—either because their own belief systems enable them to do so or because they stopped carrying around the stress of the experience when they confessed or disclosed. And because they have jettisoned the bad parts of the experience, they have allowed themselves to grow from the experience.

FIGURE 8.1 ~ Get on the Wall

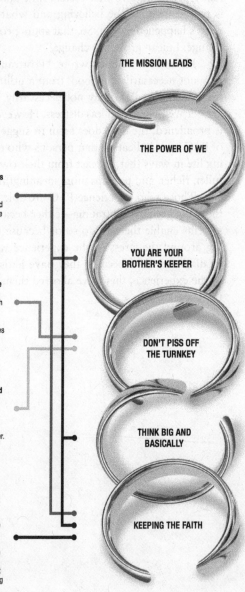

The leaders of the Hanoi Hilton POW culture asked for two things of each team member: honesty and forgiveness. In insisting on honesty, the prisoners held themselves to a high standard of conduct that few could actually attain. When they failed, they were expected to own it and move on.

Acknowledging personal failures strengthened each team member's resolve and commitment to the mission. The ability to admit failure without being rejected or condemned allowed the POWs to leave the failure behind and move forward.

Many of the POWs who became leaders (in their post-Vietnam careers) believe in the importance of giving their followers a second chance. Their POW experiences with failures and forgiveness may have helped them understand that being given a second chance often provides a powerful incentive to succeed.

The POWs insisted on sharing experiences—both successes and failures—to benefit others. All the POWs were expected to "get on the wall," share their interrogation experience, and leverage this "intelligence." Information was power.

The POWs showed little fear of failure. Perhaps their willingness to accept the risk of failure was high because they were already in a seemingly hopeless circumstance. More likely, however, it was because their culture allowed them to fail without being labeled a failure. They understood that learning from failure is the path to success. The POWs made up a learning organization that viewed failure as the price of learning how to succeed.

THE MISSION LEADS

THE POWER OF WE

YOU ARE YOUR BROTHER'S KEEPER

DON'T PISS OFF THE TURNKEY

THINK BIG AND BASICALLY

KEEPING THE FAITH

CHAPTER 9

Keeping the Faith: Creating a Culture of Hard-Nosed Optimism

In 2009, at the age of seventy, Paul Galanti was appointed commissioner of veterans services for the commonwealth of Virginia by Governor Bob McDonnell. He was the third appointee to serve in this role for a state that has the seventh largest veteran population in the nation. A total of 823,000 veterans call Virginia home. Governor McDonnell has said publicly that one of his goals is to make Virginia the most veteran-friendly state in the country. Galanti is his point man for this vision.

Virginia's Department of Veterans Services is charged with several responsibilities, including providing specialized services to Virginia's Wounded Warrior population, managing the state's veterans rehabilitative care facilities, maintaining the state's veterans cemeteries, and helping veterans apply for and obtain benefits from the federal Department of Veterans Affairs (VA). Of these four, helping veterans get earned benefits through the VA's claims process is probably the most vexing. "If you could pick one thing Paul would be most proud of, it would be the development of an automated claims processing system," explained Steve Combs, Galanti's chief of staff and director of policy.

A self-described Apple computer enthusiast and a technology early adopter, Galanti has envisioned a paperless claims processing system for more than ten years. As Combs describes it,

> Right now, we use a system that is stand-alone in each of our twenty-two field offices, and it is antiquated.

We enter data individually on a form and then click the print button and submit a hard-copy package to the VA. Then the VA takes it, and it gets either handled by paper or—if we're lucky—it gets scanned into [Adobe Acrobat] PDF form, and that's their electronic solution.

What Paul wants to do is to break through all of that by developing a system that—when submitted to the VA—would be like TurboTax, where it would flow electronically and would populate the data in a new computer system that the VA is hoping to develop and it [just] goes—electrons to electrons. No paper.

Banks do it. The IRS does it. The VA has the second largest budget of any federal agency—just after the Department of Defense. Why can't the VA do it? But changing an ingrained culture at a labyrinthine organization the size of the VA is proving harder to achieve than it sounds. Huge computer systems exist at the state and federal levels, and they don't talk to each other. When Galanti has made his case to the VA in the past, he has encountered significant resistance. Staff members at the VA have responded by saying, "We get a lot of ideas like this. They're very simplistic and they don't realize the scalability required and how large the VA is, blah, blah, blah."[1]

Galanti has heard all the excuses, but he's not giving up. He truly believes that he has the leadership support now to make it happen. The current secretary of veterans affairs, former Army Gen. Eric Shinseki, supports the initiative, and Governor McDonnell has given Galanti the authority to make it happen. Galanti is the head of a national task force of his peers, all of whom are watching his efforts closely to see if the Virginia prototype is successful and could be used as a template for other states.

Virginia has requested proposals to develop the state end of the system from potential vendors, and the VA is working in parallel at the federal level. Galanti and his team know both ends of the equation will work, but tying the two systems together will be a technical challenge. "The writing has to be done a very specific way. You run into differences between services [ranks, lexicon] and getting them lined up to speak the VA language is very difficult," Galanti says.

And, of course, getting the bureaucrats to change is the biggest challenge. Galanti continues, "It's just getting them to buy into it and making them heroes for doing it. That's how you get anything done. By letting them see the vision of just how great they're going to be once we get this thing done together and collaborate. Then, they become the most wonderful bureaucrat in the whole world if you can make this happen."[2] He's trying to give them a vision of what is possible.

A less optimistic person would have given up on this daunting and frustrating task long ago. After all, Galanti has had several careers since returning from Vietnam and says that he would be perfectly happy to be fully retired and to get back to "spoiling grandchildren."[3] But he is committed and eternally optimistic.

"Paul is the consummate gentleman and the most positive person I've ever met," Combs says. Combs points to a talk Galanti gave to some Navy chiefs in which he summarized his POW experience with three points: (1) he wasn't as tough as he thought he was; (2) there was always someone who had it worse; and (3) there's no such thing as a bad day when you have a doorknob on the inside of the door. "The key to his positiveness is that he has this amazing ability to put things in perspective," Combs adds.[4]

Researchers at the Mitchell Center for POW Studies recently completed a thirty-seven-year longitudinal study of 224 Vietnam-era POWs. They compared them to a control group of Vietnam-era non-POW aviators, looking for the keys to the remarkable resilience shown by the Hanoi Hilton prisoners. The POWs' notable story raises the question: Why do some people bounce back from adverse and traumatic experiences and suffer few, if any, long-term side effects?

Of all the factors the researchers identified, six made the final cut in affecting resilience: officer/enlisted status, age at time of capture, length of solitary confinement, low antisocial/psychopathic personality traits, low PTSD symptoms following repatriation, and optimism. Of these six variables, dispositional optimism was the strongest, most statistically significant variable. In other words, the single most important buffer against any psychiatric diagnosis was optimism—the men's positive outlook about life's inevitable curveballs. Simply put, optimists look at bad events as temporary, local, and external; pessimists look at bad events as permanent, pervasive, and personal. Optimists have perspective—some of that same perspective that age and life experience gives you. They have the ability to step back from bad and challenging events and say to themselves, "This is not going to last forever, it's not going to ruin me, and it's not my fault."

The researchers also demonstrated the benefits of optimism in everyday life and in the general population. They found that optimism can be a protective buffer against trauma and it can inoculate individuals from the medical illnesses that can result from trauma. Notably, the study's authors believe optimism can be taught; "in fact, of the six variables associated with resilience, optimism, the variable they identified as the most significant, is the only one that can be taught."[5] Optimism can consciously become a practiced behavior, one that can be internalized by individuals and organizations. In other words, it can become a cultural norm.

CREATING A CULTURE OF OPTIMISM

The Hanoi Hilton POWs systematically, thoughtfully, and incrementally created a culture of optimism—and hopefulness—in the middle of an otherwise hopeless environment. Their hope was based on commonly embraced values, some ingrained in them by their training and others by the mission they collectively adopted: Return with Honor. The Vietnam POWs' mission emphasized the importance of getting home alive, with the entire group of POWs unified and together (meaning they would not accept individual releases or releases

~ Gallows Humor: What's It Good For? ~

Orson Swindle still chuckles when he tells the story of how he convinced his interrogators that Americans celebrate a national holiday called "National Doughnut Day." This particular interrogation followed ten days of being chained to a stool with little sleep. His interrogator was being relentless in his criticisms of the United States. When he told Swindle that the United States had no valuable cultural traditions, the exhausted but angry Marine used humor to express his rage.

Swindle spontaneously spun a tall tale of National Doughnut Day. He told an elaborate story of how the United States celebrated the holiday by donning lederhosen, dancing around maypoles, and enjoying bountiful doughnuts every year on November 10.

A few months later, much to his delight, on November 10 of that year, all the POWs were served a breakfast of doughnuts—or something resembling doughnuts. While the North Vietnamese thought they were offering up a small gesture of kindness to honor the great American tradition of National Doughnut Day, Swindle and his peers delightedly knew their captors had instead honored the Marine Corps' birthday. The joke was on the North Vietnamese.[1]

Humor among the POWs has been well documented as a form of stress relief. Even the name they gave the prison—the Hanoi Hilton—reeks of sarcasm. They carried their gallows humor further by naming each cellblock after Las Vegas casinos and giving guards and interrogators names like Al Capone, Mickey Mouse, and Magoo.

The use of humor to release aggression and to encourage each other sometimes went so far that it brought retribution. When Nels Tanner confessed under severe torture that "fellow carrier pilots Lt. Cdr. Ben Casey and Lt. Clark Kent had been court-martialed for refusing to fly their missions," the Vietnamese excitedly taped the "confession" for a Japanese television program. Worldwide derision followed because the Vietnamese had not recognized Tanner's use of the fictitious names of a TV doctor and a comic book hero. Tanner spent a record 123 days in irons.

But humor was also a critically important means for relaying resistance tactics, encouraging each other, alleviating boredom, bridging isolation, and succinctly communicating leadership orders and directives. "Maintaining a sense of humor kept most of us from getting lost in self-pity," said POW Norm McDaniel. Another POW said humor gave them a way to reclaim their identity, keeping the group—and the culture they worked so hard to build—intact.[2]

---

[1] Orson Swindle, interview by the authors, September 19, 2011.
[2] Stuart I. Rochester and Frederick T. Kiley, *Honor Bound: American Prisoners of War in Southeast Asia, 1961–1973* (Annapolis, MD: U.S. Naval Institute Press, 1999), 300, 416.

in any order other than the order of capture). Led by a few SROs willing to step up and put their lives on the line, both the individuals and the collective group internalized this mission, which galvanized them and gave them hope.

For more than eight years the POWs covertly tapped out their hard-nosed optimism: "We will make it through this, together!" This behavior became habitual, a cultural norm.

THE NAVY SEALS' BIG FOUR: PUTTING RATIONAL BELIEFS INTO ACTION

The Navy SEALs use similar mental training as they prepare prospective recruits to succeed as team members. Cdr. Eric Potterat says, "We start to instill in them what we call the big four. The candidates are taught goal setting—or segmenting— arousal control, visualization, and self-talk. Those are the big four."[6]

Goal setting is simply segmenting the challenge into manageable chunks, or "eating the elephant one bite at a time," as Potterat describes it. Knowing exactly what you want as a desired outcome—as well as staying focused on what you can manage—can be a powerful antidote to despair, distraction, and disorientation.

Arousal control is learning ways to mitigate the results of the cortisol burst that can inhibit effective response to an unexpected event. Potterat uses a simple example:

> A grizzly bear walks in the room. We have that fight-or-flight response. We feel that rush, that fear, that panic. What goes on, psycho-physiologically and neuro-anatomically, is that the area of the brain called the hypothalamus communicates to the pituitary gland and releases a hormone to the adrenal cortex. The adrenals start pumping out cortisol, a stress hormone, as well as adrenaline.
>
> Once cortisol hits your bloodstream, certain things happen: vasoconstriction, blood migration

from the peripheral appendages toward the center of body organs, an increased heart rate, increased blood pressure, and muscle tension. In the grizzly bear example, I might lose an appendage, but I'm going to draw my blood to the vital organs.

Executive functions, those higher-order thought processes—planning, cognitive problem-solving abilities—they become less fine-tuned and more impaired during the fight-or-flight response. The brain essentially does a triage of what's important, and it goes into protective mode.

Cortisol then also goes to the hippocampus, an area of the brain that's responsible for memory development. In some people, it causes extreme detail-oriented memories. In others, it causes these gaps or lapses. It's just the way they defend themselves and react.

So, for the grizzly bear example, you might remember details that are phenomenal years down the line. Adaptively, your mind has processed that memory to say, "Hey, I need to remember this detail because I never want to do it again" or "I need to forget it—for protective reasons—because it was so bad."[7]

Controlling the aroused state sometimes requires reinterpreting or reframing how you view it through visualization. Dr. C. A. "Andy" Morgan, a psychiatrist at Yale's School of Medicine, has spent years studying U.S. special forces and their handling of stress. He says,

A normal person can learn fairly quickly—when taught—how to respond with less anxiety. A fancy term we use sometimes—cognitive reframing—is where we change the implication of what's happening. An anxiety disorder is people doing catastrophic thinking. They say, "Well, if this has happened, then this is going to be a disaster today." And we say, "Well, actually, no, the world doesn't come to an end." It seems so simple. With many anxiety disorders, people do these exercises with their therapist on what we call "thought stopping," or checking your thoughts and reframing the interpretation because it's the interpretation that ends up in the adrenaline or the squirt of CRF [corticotropin-releasing factor, or cortisol].[8]

Reframing is similar to the visualization technique used by athletes and doctors: mentally going through every step of a task—the perfect golf putt, the route of a successful touchdown pass, or the perfect surgical procedure down to the last suture—in hopes of further honing mental and muscle memories.

"This is stress inoculation 101," says Potterat.

Elite athletes use this beautifully. They are the true experts in the world of doing this. If I'm a swimmer and I'm at the elite level and I'm going to go into a fixed time event, we get people to visualize that event and use as many senses as possible: taste, touch, sound, sight, and smell. They taste the chlorine. They feel the water. They can hear the crowd. By the time they actually face that event—the real event—their mind has "experienced" it dozens of times, and they have less of a psychological reaction, less of a stress response. Ultimately they cope better with the real event when they have mentally rehearsed the event a number of times, all while utilizing as many senses as possible. This is true stress inoculation and leads to better coping during real events.

Self-talk, the fourth element in the Navy SEALs' big four, is based on individuals' beliefs about the situations they face and their beliefs about themselves. "What they tell themselves about a situation is going to dictate the response to the situation," says Potterat.

Your mind controls everything, right? Back to the grizzly bear example. If my belief (and self-talk) about that incident is centered around my training, my tactics, and my understanding of bear behavior (what one should and should not do), then those beliefs will affect my reactions and, ultimately, the outcome of that encounter. On the other hand, if my belief (and self-talk) leads me to believe that "It is over!" and "I'm not prepared for this," then the outcome will likely be so. So your belief system absolutely controls your fear response. There's no doubt in my mind. No doubt. Marcus Aurelius said, "Your life is what your thoughts make it." It's all about a belief system and self-talk.

How you deal with failures is a critical component of self-talk, notes Potterat.

Back to an athlete. If I'm that wide receiver who dropped a pass one day when it was third and two and we were down by six, and they just called another play to me, and my self-talk is, "Boy, I just blew that last play. I'm not sure I can do this," then guess what my performance is going to be like? As opposed to, if I'm trained and reinforced repeatedly to almost compartmentalize something bad and focus instead on my belief that I can and will catch it, my internal self-talk will be, "Throw me the ball—I will catch it."[9]

SELECTIVE AMNESIA: FOCUSING ON YOUR SUCCESSES, NOT YOUR FAILURES

West Point's Dr. Zinsser says self-talk sometimes involves forgetting failures and remembering successes. Zinsser calls it "selective amnesia." "My teacher, Bob Rotella, from Virginia, tells a wonderful story about Jack Nicklaus, the Hall of Fame golfer, giving a keynote address at a banquet," says Zinsser. "Nicklaus says, 'One of the things I'm proudest of is the way I was a clutch putter in the final round of tournaments. I have never three-putted in the final round of any tournament I've ever played.'"

Zinsser says when Nicklaus finished his speech and asked for questions, "somebody [put] their hand up and [said], 'Mister Nicklaus, nice talk. But you mentioned never having three-putted in the final round of a tournament. I have to disagree. I saw you three-putt.' To which Jack Nicklaus [replied], 'No, sir. I think you're mistaken. I have never three-putted on the final round of any tournament.' To which the guy [said], 'I've got it on videotape, Mister Nicklaus. I'd be happy to send it to you.' To which Nicklaus [said], 'No, thanks. I was there. I have never three-putted in the final round of any tournament.'"

Zinsser recounts that the questioner, after the dinner ended, ran over to Bob Rotella, who had made a name in the world of professional golf as an adviser, and said, "Doctor Rotella, please. Help me understand this. What is wrong with Nicklaus? Why won't he admit to his mistakes?"

Rotella responded, "'Well, tell me, friend, do you play the game yourself?' And the guy [said], 'Yes.' Rotella [said], 'Well, what's your handicap?' The guy [said], 'Oh, fifteen.' Meaning he's a very mediocre golfer. Then Rotella [said], 'And if you missed a lot of clutch putts, you would be inclined to remember them and sort of fall back on them.' The guy [said], 'Well, of course I would. Any normal person would do that.'"

Rotella replied to Nicklaus' questioner, "'OK. Let me get this straight. You're a fifteen handicapper and there's Nicklaus, maybe the greatest player to ever play the game, and you expect him to think like you?'"

About this anecdote Zinsser notes, "That's the deal. It's about the putter that Jack Nicklaus sees in the mirror. Now, has he three-putted in the final round of tournaments? Of course he has. But that's not the guy he sees in the mirror. You are going to have a very selective amnesia for the things that do not contribute to long-lasting confidence and focus. And you're going to have a selective memory for anything and everything that does."[10]

Letting go of failures, focusing on successes—that is what the POWs did.

USING THE GOOD PARTS TO GROW

Charlie Zuhoski stresses the need to be honest with yourself, but he adds, "Basically, this is all about picking the pieces of your past, no matter whether it was yesterday or ten years ago, and using the good parts that will help you do well, help you grow, and discarding the rest."[11] He put this philosophy to work after Vietnam. When he returned to the United States after nearly six years in captivity, he finished out his career in the Navy and went to work in 1991 as a management consultant for Booz Allen Hamilton, a government contractor that provides engineering, information technology, and management consulting services to the federal government and the private sector. By the time he retired twenty years later, in 2011, he had been promoted to the rank of partner in this publicly traded firm with more than 25,000 employees.

During the course of his career at Booz Allen, Zuhoski made his mark on one particular storied agency: the Defense Advanced Research Projects Agency (DARPA). Known for its role in inventing the Internet, DARPA is the advanced research arm of the Department of Defense whose stated mission is "Creating and Preventing Strategic Surprise." Two colleagues who worked with Zuhoski for more than a decade, Jim Kee and Allan Steinhardt, said that the veteran is responsible for growing the firm's business at DARPA over the course of two decades. How did he do it?

"Charlie was famous for saying, 'Don't ask the question if you don't want to know the answer,'" Kee, a principal at Booz Allen, said with a chuckle. "He was willing to do something that hadn't been done before." And he wasn't afraid. He consistently pursued business that others at the firm might not have. "The firm instills a certain degree of respect for lines of demarcation that Charlie just didn't have," Vice President Steinhardt explained.[12] He simply wasn't afraid to color outside the lines. It wasn't that he was breaking rules or advocated doing so; he just pushed the envelope—especially if it benefited his clients and helped to grow the firm's business.

And grow the business he did. "Out of the prison experience, you do have time to contemplate," Zuhoski says. "You are free of the politics of life." He carries that freedom with him to this day. "The [political] pressures of life today in business cloud many people," Zuhoski says. "I just strive and have no fear of politics. . . . I've lost only one recompete [that is, a rebid for a project at the end of a contract term] at DARPA. And this was due in large part to politics. The winner also used one of our staff in their proposal as a key person—without confirming that the individual would change companies."[12]

A "key person" named in a proposal must be assigned to the project if the company wins the contract. Listing a competitor's employee as potential member of the proposed project team—in effect, poaching the employee—was not illegal but could be considered unethical. Zuhoski says, "I happened to mention it to the director of DARPA, who offered to look into it, as the contract was for one of the office directors." The veteran thought about it. He had a case for an official complaint, and his client was willing to go out on a limb for him. But he decided that the long-term value of the relationship was more important and that although this setback loomed large at the time, it could ultimately be a chance to regroup, learn, and come back to the client even stronger. He was optimistic, confident his team could reclaim the project at the end of the next contract term. So, "I told [my client] that I didn't want to embarrass the office director and wanted to drop it. Rather than hand-wringing over how we were 'cheated,' we set about the task of winning back the contract in four years, first by providing the best turnover we could to the winning contractor."[13] His team won the next recompete four years later.

THE MENTAL EDGE: THE KEY TO HIGH PERFORMANCE

Away from the interrogations, goal setting, visualization, arousal control, and self-talk all came together in establishing the POWs' daily cultural norms. George Coker notes that

Stockdale "set the pace" for all the other POWs. Stockdale later wrote of how he personally prepared for torture sessions with a combination of the SEALs' big four: "Power as a political prisoner comes from building layer upon layer of convictions that are hard to assail. You lie awake at night memorizing and concentrating on position points that you can maintain for hours, eyeball to eyeball with your interrogator, not blinking or betraying fear or guilt; yes, and position points you can maintain on the ropes. Because on all important issues, unless you fold, those ropes are going to come. And as we all know, that's serious business, for it's in the ropes that death visited some."[14]

Stockdale also wrote, "I used to perform a ritualistic chant under my breath as I was marched to the interrogation room with a bayonet pricking the middle of my back: 'Show no fear, show no fear; don't let your eyes show fear.'"[15] In his visualization and self-talk, he found the strength to keep going back for more.

Lt. Cdr. Josh Butner, former director of professional education at the Naval Special Warfare Center, says that the mental edge is what separates high performers from others. "It's all mental. You can take any kid with an ounce of physical ability, and you can turn him into a SEAL, if he's got the heart," notes Commander Butner. "It really doesn't matter the physical capability. Because the human body—and that's what we prove to them going through BUDS—we prove to them that the human body is incredibly resilient. It all starts with the mind and the heart. If you decide, that's what it's all about—the willpower."[16] Turns out this is what makes a "successful" POW as well.

And this is where age and experience become your allies. "The best predictor of future behavior is past behavior," says Potterat. In other words, if someone has navigated through adversity successfully before in their lives, there's a strong likelihood that they're going to navigate successfully again.[17]

FIGURE 9.1 ~ Keeping the Faith

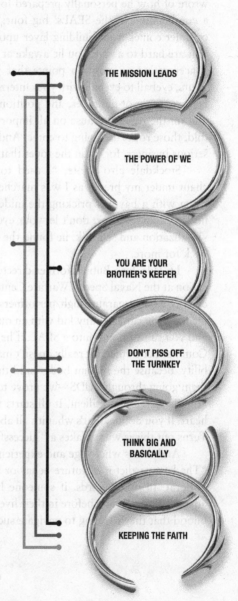

The POWs' hard-nosed optimism grew to become systemic. Nearly all the POWs recall times when they were down and a cellmate or the man on the other side of the wall picked them up and helped them regain their belief that they would survive and accomplish their mission. They collectively modeled and tried to teach all the newcomers the mindset that they were going to make it through their ordeal.

The POWs focused their mental energy on what they wanted to achieve. Much like championship athletes, they spent time visualizing their success, working through the steps to success, and preparing for the scenarios they might face. By focusing their mental energy, they reduced their stress, increased their resolve, and increased their odds of successfully handling a situation if they eventually faced it.

Time to think was critical to their success. Stockdale wrote of time spent "building layer upon layer of convictions" in order to withstand torture. Many POWs write and speak of time they spent evaluating what mattered in their life. They turned their isolation to their own benefit, and they developed resolve about what mattered to them.

THE MISSION LEADS

THE POWER OF WE

YOU ARE YOUR BROTHER'S KEEPER

DON'T PISS OFF THE TURNKEY

THINK BIG AND BASICALLY

KEEPING THE FAITH

CHAPTER 10

The Power of We:
The Value of a Social Network

It was a cold morning on February 7, 1971, when several of the POWs—James Stockdale, Robbie Risner, George Coker, and Vernon Ligon—decided to push the limits of their resistance to date by holding a large and loud church service. In the months leading up to this particular incident, services—part patriotic and part religious—had been held on a regular basis, even though the prisoners had been banned from holding organized meetings and had been warned of retaliation by their captors. For this service, the POWs went one step further and alerted their captors in advance of their intention to hold another service. The event was the culmination and combination of long pent-up frustration and a new sense of confidence brought on by the move to Camp Unity.

By early 1970 the POWs—some of whom had been in captivity for nearly six years—had experienced a big change in their living conditions. As a result of the recent Son Tay raid, the North Vietnamese were spooked. Even though the raid had been unsuccessful, the Vietnamese were worried that U.S. forces might attack all their prison camps. By bringing all the POWs to one location, they could more easily defend a subsequent rescue attempt by the Americans.

Consequently, the POWs were moved into one prison camp, a place they called Camp Unity. This consolidation was an emotional reunion for many of the prisoners who, to date, had been able to communicate only through walls. Some of them had never even met each other. They were still divided into separate rooms, but each room held thirty to forty men. In addition, the prisoners were allowed to exercise, bathe, and communicate in even larger groups. They were like kids in a candy store: for the first time since they had been captured, they were able to really socialize. The confusion and emotions associated with these newfound freedoms unified them, but they also emboldened them.

Although the restrictions placed on them had been loosened, their captors still refused to accord the men the international rights and recognition they were entitled to as POWs. In other words, their captors still called them war criminals and treated them as such. This derision, combined with the prisoners' newfound power in numbers, made a confrontation with the captors all the more likely. And so, the POWs began hosting a weekly church service in direct violation of a ban on organized meetings. In Rochester and Kiley's book *Honor Bound*, Stockdale characterized the act as particularly defiant: "'The Communists could accept our milling around a cell block and talking to each other in private conversations,' Stockdale said, 'but for a single American to stand before a group and lead a prayer, or for a trio to stand before the group and sing a hymn, was a provocative act.'"[1]

On this particular winter morning in 1971, whether consciously or not, the POWs took advantage of an opportunity to test the efficacy and unity of their organization, its mission, and its well-ingrained culture of behavior. They staged what they later called the "church riot."

After their first assembly on December 27, 1970, the men had been threatened with torture and deprivation. But Camp Unity and the safety in numbers afforded them by their new living arrangements had only reinforced their organization's strength. They decided to push the limits even further, and Ligon informed the captors of the prisoners' intent to hold services again on February 7.

Because of his knowledge of the Bible and his expert speaking skills, Coker was selected to be the chaplain. The

~ The Son Tay Raid ~

Carried out by more than fifty U.S. commandos on the morning of November 21, 1970, and backed by more than a hundred aircraft and three aircraft carriers, the Son Tay raid was a plan to rescue an estimated seventy to eighty POWs held at the Son Tay prison camp, a remote compound located twenty-three miles west of Hanoi.

The rescue attempt failed because the prisoners who had been there—the actual number was fewer than sixty—had been moved elsewhere four months earlier. The move had gone undetected by U.S. intelligence.

Special operations forces executed the well-rehearsed insertion flawlessly and only encountered resistance at a second location four hundred meters away. They emerged from the brief battle with no loss of life, while the enemy took heavy casualties; estimates range from two dozen to more than a hundred. The U.S. forces were able to search the camp thoroughly before leaving by helicopter; they spent a total of thirty minutes on the ground. Still, it was considered an intelligence failure.

The result is the instructional part of the story. Fearing other rescue attempts, the North Vietnamese consolidated most of the POWs in North Vietnam into the Hanoi Hilton itself—to shore up their defenses. For the first time, most of the American POWs were in one place at the same time. The increased population overcrowded the prison camp, but now, the prisoners were able to collaborate and socialize. True mission solidarity came within the grasp of those willing and able to exploit it.

Being together and being crowded presented challenges, but the ease of communication; the ability to pass orders along quickly, learn from each other, and boost each other's morale; and the sense of unity all brought renewed and increased solidarity. The Son Tay raid set the stage for the POWs' final victories as a high-performance culture.

prisoners assembled a small choir of six men, who began to practice in anticipation of the event. Risner was selected to give the benediction. Tensions ran high in the organization, as the POWs knew they would face repercussions for the act of defiance. But they had a plan to mitigate the effects: "Every portion of the service was to have a different leadership. The opening prayer would be said by one man, the choir of six would sing, the scripture was to be given by a different person, and the thought for the day by yet another person. We also had a contingency plan: to prevent violence Vern [Ligon], if he felt it best, could call the whole thing off. If they pulled out the leaders, we agreed that we would continue until the last junior officer was left alone." By dividing up the responsibility, they would force their captors to punish all or none.[2]

The morning of February 7, 1971, came, and the Vietnamese were lying in wait right outside the door when the fifteen-minute service commenced. They barged into the room and demanded that the choir stop singing. They didn't. They told Coker to stop talking. He continued. Howie Rutledge quoted some scripture, and he was told to stop. He didn't. Coker began the benediction, and another guard came forward and demanded that he stop. Instead, he finished. When Ligon dismissed the service at its conclusion, the entire assembled group began to disperse, and the guards immediately rounded up Risner, Coker, and Rutledge and took them outside into the courtyard to mete out their punishment.

Then it got interesting. According to Risner, "It was only a few seconds until Maj. Bud Day, one of the toughest men I know, started singing 'The Star-Spangled Banner,' with everyone joining in. I have never heard a sound like it. We had not heard 'The Star-Spangled Banner' during all those years, except in our own minds or under our breath. Now, though, it was ringing throughout the camp, over the wall, and into the city of Hanoi. It lifted up everyone in the whole stinking camp!"[3]

Just before dark later that day, the "riot" continued. Risner writes, "Singing started again from Building Seven. They sang other songs in addition to the 'Star-Spangled Banner.' To top it off, they concluded with: 'This is Building Number Seven, Number Seven, Number Seven. This is Building Number Seven. Where the Hell is Number One?' That started a chant around the camp. Every single building, some with which we had had limited or no contact, picked it up until the whole camp joined in. It so shook the Vietnamese that they called out the riot squad!"[4]

Nothing in the camp would ever be the same again. If an organization is only as strong as its weakest link, this chain—the organization and the culture the prisoners had built—had proved unbreakable that day. The POWs' ability to resist their captors had been tested for many years, and their defiance was like a well-exercised muscle with memory. This time, their unity had been tested. They successfully stood up as a group to their captors and beat them at their own game.

They were punished for hosting the church services. Several of the men were put in leg irons for days at a time. But the Vietnamese acquiesced and let them continue their weekly religious meetings. It was a tangible victory. Indeed, according to Risner, "Up to then we had never been permitted to have any part in any of the decision making. We were controlled like animals—when we went to bed, when we got up, when we ate, when we finished, when we went to empty our buckets, when we bathed—everything was controlled by the Vietnamese. Now they felt they were losing this control."[5]

The lessons of solidarity stayed with the POWs, even as their conditions improved. Instead of relaxing their attention to their mission as it became clear that they were going to make it home (even if it was not clear when they would go home), many of them intensified their focus. They found both strength and meaning in solidarity—"the power of we."

Paul Galanti put it bluntly: "We were an organization of 'we's' in Hanoi. We didn't have any idea what anybody looked like. We couldn't tell if somebody had a southern accent. We all tapped the same way and all sounded the same—except for the Air Force guys [who] misspelled a lot of words. We were a whole lot of we because we were all in the same boat. We are going to get through it together, or else." This culture of unity—the power of we—had matured and become so strong that it was unstoppable.[6]

~ The Hanoi Hilton Bell Curve ~

George Coker was the youngest member of the Alcatraz Gang—the POWs sent in 1967 to a special prison near Hoa Lo for more than two years because the North Vietnamese considered them troublemakers. James Stockdale, another member, considered the men in the Alcatraz Gang his closest allies in establishing the cultural norms needed to successfully achieve the mission. As Stockdale noted, "I thought of them as my leaders—don't ever forget that one man's troublemaker is another man's leader, and vice versa."[1]

Coker had an insider's look at how Stockdale, Robbie Risner, Jeremiah Denton, and other SROs viewed the Alcatraz Gang and its mission. Coker understands that the POW organization was like any group of people trying to achieve a mission. The men's efforts and abilities fell along the familiar bell curve. High achievers formed the high end of the curve, and low achievers formed the low end. Most were in the middle. Coker succinctly captures how the organizational mission, values, structure, and daily function interacted in this bell curve:

"There were, interestingly, exactly eleven men at the top of the bell curve, and eleven at the bottom of the bell curve," notes Coker. "We eventually got all but two of the ones at the low end to join us."

At the high end of the bell curve, anchoring its performance demands, Coker cites Stockdale, Risner, and Denton as the three who set the pace for the POW culture and organizational standards. They set the high end of the bell curve beyond what many POWs may have first thought was possible.

"I don't think you can quite comprehend the fear level. It's pretty hard to say, 'That guy wasn't tough enough.' But, unfortunately, there was a line," says Coker.

It was way above any standard performance line, but the fear caused some to back down. People like Stockdale and Risner—when it came to pure bullheadedness—stand out. Time and again—no matter how badly they got beat, they would go back in. They could be down for a day, a week, or a month, but when they got their strength back, they stood up and got punched in the face full blown again. Such courage: to

(continued)

overcome your fear and set an example, to do what you know you need to do, even though you pay a price.

Sometimes circumstances can move the middle of the bell curve. Coker believes the POW organization found its own inner strength when he and other Alcatraz Gang members were pulled out and sent to an isolated prison camp. He says, "[The organization] was definitely damaged. But if [the separation] did not encourage [the organization] to grow, it did inject it with a new sense of purpose and even courage. They could say, 'They stood up to the end. They stood up all the way to the end.' Now, these individual pockets out there could say, 'I can stand up to that, too.'"[2]

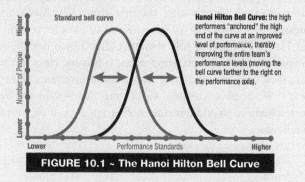

FIGURE 10.1 ~ The Hanoi Hilton Bell Curve

---

[1] James Bond Stockdale, *Thoughts of a Philosophical Fighter Pilot* (Stanford, CA: Hoover Institution Press, 1995), 141.

[2] George Coker, interview by the authors, December 4, 2011.

THE "KISSINGER 20": REFUSING FREEDOM UNTIL THE MISSION IS ACCOMPLISHED

Fast-forward two years to February 1973. Few stories capture the essence of the impact of the Hanoi Hilton culture better than the story of the "Kissinger 20."

One of the most basic tenets of Return with Honor was that the POWs would not accept early release. The rules of the road were that they would return home in the order they were shot down. Nobody was to accept early release because the Vietnamese could use this tactic for propaganda purposes or to manipulate the POWs. Only prisoners who were seriously injured could accept early release.

As the first batch of Hanoi Hilton POWs to be released was considered, Ed Mechenbier found himself bumped off the list of early returnees in order to make way for POWs with serious injuries. He was instead added to the second group being released. Shortly after the first group left, Mechenbier and nineteen other POWs were moved to another section of the Hanoi Hilton and told they would be flown out the following day. As they compared notes, it became clear to them that they were not the ones who should have been released next. "We knew something was wrong. We should not have been scheduled to go home for another ten days or so," recalls Mechenbier.

So we refused to put on our clothes. We refused to leave.

For five days, there was this dickering back and forth. Every day, the Vietnamese would come in and tell us to put our clothes on; they weren't about to torture us to make us go home. On the fifth day, an Air Force brigadier general came into the camp. He talked to Col. Norm Gaddis, the senior American officer left behind. The American general could only talk to the senior POW. The American general convinced Colonel Gaddis it was a legitimate release.

He did not know all the details of it, but it was not a propaganda ploy by the Vietnamese. With that, Colonel Gaddis came to our cell and told us, "I don't know what is going on, but the senior ranking officer of the delegation is here to get us out of here, and he says it is a legitimate release. Will you go home now?"

We said, "No, we're not going to go home. It's not the way the protocol was read to us, and after all these years, we're not about to compromise ourselves for a few days' earlier release." With that, Colonel Gaddis went down the line, and he gave each one of us a direct verbal order: "You will leave today on my authority." He went through all twenty of us individually.

So, we put on our clothes, and we told the Vietnamese that if we see so much as one camera, hear so much as one click, we're turning around and going back into the cell. They let us march out in formation, we got on the bus, and went to the airport on the eighteenth of February, and there, according to the protocols, we were released.

As we're going to the airport, we see the C-141 land. Our bus goes down a side road to a Vietnamese fighter squadron building. There was candy and fruits and decorations on the table. The Vietnamese told us our airplane had been delayed, so we should refresh ourselves for our trip.

We knew they were going to use it for a propaganda thing, so we just filed into the first few rows of the seats in this squadron theater, and we just sat there. The Vietnamese entreated us several times to have something before our long trip. We just sat there. They finally decided that our airplane had arrived.

I get on the airplane, and I sit down next to a portly American with a crew cut, thick glasses, and a black suit. I put my hand out and say, "Hi, I'm Ed Mechenbier." [And] he says, "I'm Dr. Roger Shields. It is my job to get you guys out of here. What the hell have you guys been doing for five days?"[7]

As it turned out, when Henry Kissinger went to Hanoi after the first round of POWs were sent home, the Vietnamese gave him a list of the next 112 men scheduled to be released. They said that as a goodwill gesture, they would release twenty people early. Henry Kissinger did not know he should have circled the next twenty names on the list. Instead, he went down through the list and randomly circled the names of twenty men—regardless of their shoot-down date.

Place yourself in the POWs' shoes for a moment. You have spent up to seven years with filth, deprivation, isolation, and torture. Your family, freedom, and future are all just hours and steps away. All you have to do is walk out to it and accept the ride back to freedom. The temptation to ignore that final propaganda skirmish and just run for the plane pulls at you.

After years of incarceration, the POWs in the Kissinger 20 chose to stand by their group credo and mission, despite the temptation. As Zinsser points out, a human adversary or enemy is not required for the power of we: "There are surrogates for a human adversary that can serve as a unifier of purpose for members of a team or group."[8] Zinsser cites a commonly embraced goal as a positive surrogate for an adversary. Shared external (nonhuman) adversity, limited resources, and numerous other obstacles and hardships also can become a common adversary.

The POWs essentially told the Vietnamese how and when they would leave, refusing to take the propaganda bait. Even with the finish line in sight, the smell of freedom tantalizingly close, they refused to leave their duty posts until they were absolutely certain their mission had been accomplished.

FIGURE 10.2 ~ The Power of We

The ownership of the mission became so personal that SROs had to order some POWs to stand down once it became clear that they had accomplished their mission. The Kissinger 20 had to be ordered to board the plane. They delayed claiming their freedom because of their commitment to their collective mission. The psychological motivation to accomplish their mission proved to be even more powerful than their own well-being and the fruit of their success—going home.

"The power of we" became one of the critical catalysts for the POW culture. Although they held diverse worldviews and personal beliefs and even widely differing opinions about their daily orders, they shared a common adversary. But a human adversary or enemy is not required for the power of we.

The Hanoi Hilton POWs understood and capitalized on the power of we. When they sensed that their captors could no longer afford to seriously harm them, they ramped up their efforts to include public displays of resistance. With a clear understanding that some of them would pay a price for the church service, the POWs played their hand for maximum benefit.

THE MISSION LEADS

THE POWER OF WE

YOU ARE YOUR BROTHER'S KEEPER

DON'T PISS OFF THE TURNKEY

THINK BIG AND BASICALLY

KEEPING THE FAITH

How High-Performance Teams Are Built

No case study of a successful organization is complete without some attempt to draw conclusions about how the lessons learned in building that group can be applied to other organizations. Most of the lessons are readily apparent in the stories told by the POWs or in the stories told about them by their associates in their subsequent careers.

Still, there is a danger in accepting the obvious. The obvious can sometimes mask the more important lesson. Many times in interviews even the POWs shrugged at what they did and attributed their unusual performance to their military background or their life-and-death situation. Similarly, their age and education are often cited as the reasons their performance was so exceptional. Clearly, these factors all played some role in how they created their high-performance team. But the obvious answers miss more important takeaways.

MANY COULD ... BUT FEW DO

There are hundreds, even thousands, of organizations in cities around the world that have equally bright, disciplined, educated, and ambitious professionals filling their ranks. By almost any standard—mental, physical, psychological, moral, or ethical—numerous organizations match up to the POWs on paper.

But at the end of the day, only a handful of organizations come close to the POWs' performance level. Most organizations eventually succumb to the "every man for himself" philosophy that was the undoing of POW camps in previous wars. Even a casual perusal of POW literature from other wars shows that military training, rank, education, and age do not guarantee stellar behavior when service members are thrust into the crucible of a POW camp. Indeed, far from increasing the likelihood of selfless behavior, the stress of prison and life-and-death challenges seems to diminish the likelihood of looking out for a group's best interests.

~ The Fourth Allied POW Wing ~

As the middle years of torture and isolation in the Hanoi Hilton gave way to the final years, the SROs used the larger groups and better communication in Camp Unity to restore some of the cultural norms of military life. Air Force colonel John Peter Flynn, the highest-ranking officer in the Hanoi Hilton at that time, created the "Fourth Allied POW Wing" and assigned other SROs as "headquarters staff."

There still is debate among former POWs as to whether the designation of the Fourth Allied POW Wing served much purpose and whether the formalizing of command hierarchy had much daily impact on an already functional organizational culture. In the end, creation of the wing may have served two important functions: it provided structure for later accountability for the pilots' conduct as POWs and for future preservation of the legacy they created.

The wing implemented traditional military fitness reports, decorations and awards, and other management tools of military life, all of which proved important years later. George Coker recalls working with some of the SROs after repatriation, as they wrote performance evaluations for each POW in the wing. Coker recalls, "One guy specifically asked Stockdale why he couldn't get the job he wanted." The answer was found in the POW's fitness report—his military job performance review. While he had done nothing wrong as a POW, neither had he performed exceptionally.

Perhaps as importantly, after repatriation the term "Fourth Allied POW Wing" grew to symbolize the prisoners' victory against all odds. Decades later the four simple words still summarize their mission, their solidarity, their perseverance, and their victory. For future POWs, the moniker serves as a reminder that duty and honor are never imprisoned.

Even if you remove the duress of prison life, education alone cannot explain the Hanoi Hilton high-performance phenomenon, or many universities would be high-performance utopias. Age alone cannot explain it, or organizations with older workers would prove to be just as agile and adaptive as their younger competitors and would consistently outperform them.

HOW EFFECTIVE TEAMS ARE MADE

To understand how the Hanoi Hilton POWs achieved high performance, it is helpful to turn to Dr. Bruce Tuckman's theory of how effective teams are formed.

Fresh out of Princeton with his doctorate in psychology, Tuckman first spelled out his theory on small group formation in 1965 in a short article written after spending two years as a research psychologist at the Naval Medical Research Institute in Bethesda, Maryland. While his professional life has primarily been invested in educational psychology, his group formation theory has grown to be among the best-known business school models for studying how effective teams form.

The stages Tuckman identified are "forming" (orientation to group function and boundaries, as well as determining who fits on the team), "storming" (often turbulent negotiation over what the team is about and whether and where individual views fit in), "norming" (establishing the team rules and where individuals fit in), and "performing" (actually accomplishing what the team set out to do).[1]

The POWs went through an iteration of Tuckman's process as they created their own society and culture, and they continued to encounter forming and storming tensions throughout their years of imprisonment, as new shoot-downs (actually a new generation of bomber and fighter pilots) entered the Hanoi Hilton system. They also had to deal with dissenters within the POW organization, that is, cellmates who disagreed with the mission.

Some organizational experts believe the first two items in Tuckman's theory—forming and storming—take up 60–70 percent of a team's time. Most of the time and resources will be consumed in getting the right people on the team and fighting through all the different ideas and perspectives to reach common ground about what the team's mission will be. But once those two issues are settled—who is on the bus and where it is headed—the creation of cultural norms and the actual performance of the mission are often relatively straightforward.

The POWs formed a high-performance team against formidable odds: the daily Hanoi Hilton environment. Every day was filled with uncertainty and lack of control. They lived for days, weeks, and months at a time in stifling boredom and dreary isolation with occasional moments of sheer terror, fear, and unfathomable psychological and physical pain.

The magnitude of what they accomplished collectively is difficult to overstate. They achieved a professional standard of conduct that makes other professionals in tough jobs—even Navy SEALs—look on in awe. The answer to how they did it is found in the culture they formed, a culture that they sustained across concrete walls, geographic distances, and several years.

THE FORMING PHASE

If you can choose who is on your team, you already have more control than the POWs had in their forming process. You can screen for all the factors you believe are important to achieving your organizational mission. Education, psychological profile, and life experience can all be considered in your selection process. Finding team members who, like these aviators, display high levels of affiliation and achievement in their personality profiles may give you an edge in creating a high-performance team. Collecting a team of optimists—people who understand that setbacks are temporary, local, and external—can also offer an edge. At the same time, Stockdale would recommend avoiding the simple optimist who denies the reality of his or her plight. Look for those who can acknowledge the setbacks without accepting them as permanent or fatal. Similarly, high-performance teams can benefit from having members with much life experience—people who have the age and wisdom that comes from successfully catching and returning life's curveballs. Regardless of what today's human resources departments may say, younger is not always better. Conversely, age is not a proof of wisdom or resilience. Life experience is what matters.

At the other end of the spectrum, if you cannot control who is on your team—which is often the case in public sector and union jobs, as well as in many nonprofits and community organizations—you are no worse off than the POWs. You can still focus on finding a core group that will agree on the organization's values, commonly embraced mission, and rules of the road for achieving the mission. Find ways to work around the outliers at the lower end of the performance bell curve. Focus energy on moving as many adopters as possible into the high end of the bell curve. Focus your resources and energy on what is truly in your control.

THE STORMING PHASE

The POWs had some input at the second stage of Tuckman's high-performance team creation theory: the storming process. They could and did debate over their mission, goals, standards, norms, and chain of command. There were lengthy debates about who held rank over whom, whether escape was a wise course of action, and whether hunger strikes (which were ordered on several occasions by SROs) were punishment for them or their captors. In short, the storming process of their formation proved that they were not all saints or automatons. They faced disagreement, disillusionment, and dissension within their ranks. They had—and have—feet of clay.

Their storming process was not short-circuited by rank, deadlines, or policy and procedure manuals. Stockdale himself expressed thankfulness that they were out of reach of bureaucrats and experts in Washington. They used this isolation to their advantage, working through their challenges by themselves, one tap code message at a time, one torture session at a time, one minute at a time. Instead of hurting them, the isolation and the lack of a highly systematized infrastructure to examine their common plight and their shared values in depth were viewed as a challenge.

THE NORMING PHASE

Organizations that want to perform at an exceptional level need to devote significant resources to finding their commonly held core values. Ed Mechenbier said that the POWs "left our egos at the door," even though doing so was "a tough thing for fighter pilots to do."[2] They were able get to their bedrock values and focus on succeeding at their mission. One tap at a time, they confirmed their shared core values, set up guidelines for how they would live by those values, and then quietly and patiently perpetuated and defended those values. That is how they won their war.

The guidelines that shepherded the POWs' daily behavior helped with the norming process that Tuckman describes. In an organization like the Hanoi Hilton POWs', these guidelines allowed cultural norms to permeate up, down, and across the organizational chart. They became systemic. Mechenbier tells of an interrogation session that started out simply enough but became a point of solidarity for the POWs when it resulted in a beating:

> At one point, the Vietnamese hauled me in, and we had an interrogation. They were making disparaging comments about my wife. They were making things up: "She's seeing other men, she's had babies," all kinds of stuff. I shot back, "You shouldn't judge American women by Vietnamese standards." The interrogator said, "What does that mean?" I said, "That might be common in your culture when the man goes away, but not in my house."
>
> OK, they beat the crap out of me for that. The first thing you did when you got back to your room was tap out what it was [what the interrogation session

was about]. Most of the time, it was just a BSQ—a bullshit quiz. But I let them know I had gotten beaten up for what the Vietnamese considered an inappropriate comment.

Within a week, three or four other guys went in and did the same thing. The Vietnamese were using the same interrogation technique, so our guys used the same response back.

It did two things. First, it said, "We're willing to go to bat and not let one guy hang out there for a comment, no matter how flippant." And the other thing was it told the Vietnamese that we were hanging together, we were communicating, and we saw the value of presenting a common front. Those are the little things that make you realize that we aren't signing an oath in blood, but we are in fact acting in concert and we are in fact a team.[3]

Some of the values developed by the POWs will be common in most high-performance teams. Topping that list is a high sense of personal responsibility, nurtured by an environment that grants team members the personal autonomy and authority necessary to carry out responsibility. Second-guessing decisions made by team members after insisting that they take responsibility is deadly. The POW structure gave the prisoners the right to decide how much torture they could take. Their isolation forced them to make critical decisions without approval or policy manual consultation. Each POW's judgment was trusted; they were guided only by their general rules of the road. The only steadfast rule was that they be honest with other POWs about their behavior. They grew to insist on no excuses, no dishonesty, no second-guessing. They readily offered second chances while insisting that all team members learn from their failures.

Most high-performance teams accept failure as the price of success. Groups that make few or no mistakes are not innovating and learning enough. Within the Hanoi Hilton, they learned from their failures. Failure was forgiven while the lessons learned were carried forward. And the individual was redeemed. Failures that lead to organizational growth rarely sideline careers in high-performance teams.

These teams are also driven to communicate. Rather than hoarding and compartmentalizing knowledge to become more powerful, high-performance team members disseminate it as a valuable resource to be shared and leveraged. Communication in high-performance teams does not move down from the top. It moves laterally, team member to team member, or cell to cell, as in the POWs' case. It reflects encouragement, challenge, competition, analytical thinking, sharing of knowledge, and the ever-critical element of humor.

Another common characteristic of high-performance teams is a balance between the focus on the collective mission and attention to personal interests. Team members focus on the mission, while team leaders focus on making sure team members are protected, are nurtured, and have the resources they need to accomplish the mission. The high-performance team pyramid can often look inverted.

THE PERFORMING PHASE

Much of the daily performing—that is, moment-by-moment decisions and behavior—of the high-performance POW team

~ When Somebody Pursues a Different Mission ~

John Dramesi, as the SRO in a cell of eight men, convinced one cellmate to join him in an escape attempt in 1969. The other six believed the attempt would not succeed, and they proved correct. Dramesi and his escape partner, Edwin L. Atterberry, were quickly recaptured—only twelve hours and three miles later. Atterberry died from the brutal punishment inflicted on him upon his recapture by the North Vietnamese, but Dramesi survived the beatings.

All the POWs in the camp shared in the ensuing retribution as their captors tried to uncover details of how the escape was carried out and to discourage

(continued)

subsequent attempts. Many of the POWs questioned whether the escape attempt was worth it. Over time the camp reached the consensus that it was fruitless for Caucasian POWs to try to escape in the heart of the capital city of an Asian country. Their likelihood of successfully finding freedom was far outweighed by the risks.

Regardless of the escape's outcome, Dramesi and Atterberry clearly knew that the hundreds of POWs who did not attempt escape, who remained behind, would suffer the consequences of the escapees' actions. Because of the brutal, prison-wide punishment for this offense, individual escape attempts—although mandated by the military's Code of Conduct—became a lower priority than the mission of getting everybody home alive with their honor intact.

Dramesi, however, continued to disagree with the leadership's priorities. He believed escape was the prisoners' duty and the highest form of resistance, successful or not. Simply put, he had a different mission and focus than the rest of the POWs.

When he pushed for a second escape attempt in 1972, while peace negotiations to end the war were under way, his SROs faced a dilemma. Dramesi could—and did—point to the Code of Conduct as his marching orders. Dramesi was demanding to be allowed to do something that jeopardized the greater mission but that he had a legal right to do.

The POW leadership had a dilemma and debate ensued. "There was a lot of gamesmanship," says George Coker. "You had somebody with the right idea, and others who were willing to go—there were real plans—but in the final analysis, the risk far outweighed the gain."

POW leaders allowed Dramesi to spend months planning what he considered a viable escape as long as an SRO could make the final decision on the plan's implementation. When he presented his plan to the SRO, it was quashed, and Dramesi begrudgingly obeyed the orders to stand down.

"What does a CEO do when the plan does not look workable? You cancel it outright, or send them back to the drawing board," says Coker. "Some of that may have been gamesmanship, because they knew there was no way he was going to get there because of limited knowledge and capabilities. In the end, they made the decision it was so nonviable that it was not worth the risk."[1]

Dramesi obeyed the order but disagrees with his SRO's decision to this day.[2] Ultimately, the leaders decided to keep energies focused on the mission of returning everybody home safely—a mission that served the greater good of the organization, not the ambitions of one member.

---

[1] George Coker, interview by the authors, December 4, 2011.
[2] The authors contacted Mr. Dramesi for comment and contribution to this story, and he reiterated his persistent belief that he should have been granted permission to stage a second escape attempt. He would agree to be interviewed only if he could control the direction and focus of the book. The authors declined.

was filtered through two Stoic philosophy and sports psychology dictums: understand what you can and cannot control and focus your energy only on what you can control. Specifically, the prisoners were expected to observe the following guidelines: Refuse to be distracted by what you cannot control and by what does not move you toward your mission. Guard against mission creep. Measure the resources required to control something, and weigh that cost against the return. Continually assess and reassess what you are doing against its effectiveness in reaching your goal. Be a learning organization. Be willing to accept mistakes as the price of learning. Forgive yourself and others for mistakes made, and make sure you learn from them. Finally, provide an environment of control, inclusion, and openness where individuals can find the time and safety to examine their fears and learn to lean into them.

NO ADJOURNING ALLOWED:
A SUSTAINING CULTURE

Years after publishing his "forming-storming-norming-performing" theory of high-performance teams, Tuckman added a fifth step: adjourning. After completing their mission, most high-performance teams adjourn—or disband. But the POWs did not.

Twenty-four years after the POWs were repatriated, one of them returned to Vietnam—as the U.S. ambassador to Hanoi. In addition to being a former POW, Pete Peterson was a retired Air Force colonel and a former member of the U.S. House of Representatives. When Ambassador Bill Richardson approached him in 1997 and said that President Clinton wanted him to be the first U.S. ambassador to Vietnam since American troops had left the country, the irony wasn't lost on anyone. The Clinton administration's goal was to normalize relations and improve bilateral trade. The appointment was controversial, as many in the United States were adamantly opposed to the move. Many Vietnam veterans, South

Vietnamese immigrants now living in the United States, and politicians were hard and fast against opening diplomatic relations with Vietnam.

But Peterson felt otherwise. "I went back to Vietnam not because I had to, but because I wanted to. I saw the Vietnamese at their very worst and they saw me at my very worst as well," he explained at a congressional hearing in the spring of 1998. "It's a rare opportunity for someone to go back to a country like this in which there was so much pain and to focus on the future—not the past."[4]

Peterson understood that Vietnam was the twelfth most populous nation in the world and that 60 percent of the population was under the age of twenty-five. For the Vietnamese, the war he had fought against their government was ancient history. He saw the potential for American products and influence. Much like China, Vietnam had a communist government, but it also had a nation that was hungry for capitalism. Peterson said, "They essentially woke up one morning and said, 'This is what we have to do. We have to make the transition from a centrally planned economy to a free market economy if we are going to be successful in the rest of the world.'"[5] Peterson saw it as his mission to help. In his opinion, it was the right and honorable thing to do.

One of his major goals during his tenure in North Vietnam was to obtain a waiver to the Jackson-Vanik Amendment. Originally enacted into federal law in 1974 and named after its cosponsors, Senator Henry M. "Scoop" Jackson of Washington and Representative Charles Vanik of Ohio, this amendment was intended to punish countries with nonmarket economies that restricted emigration. It denied most-favored-nation status to these countries, effectively limiting trade between them and the United States. However, the president could issue an annual waiver to the amendment, as was done for China in the late 1970s. Peterson wanted a waiver for Vietnam, and he fought hard for it.

Vietnam veterans in Congress argued over the merit of renewing the waiver and debated the value of opening up a new market for U.S. business and the fallout of essentially rewarding a communist country with most-favored-nation status. Senator Bob Smith of New Hampshire summarized the opposition succinctly in his 1998 congressional testimony: "I believe American businesses should invest in struggling democracies in Asia. We don't need to encourage them to invest in communist dictatorships where basic human rights are still being denied."[6] But Peterson framed the debate differently. He saw it as a continuation of his long-term mission, Return with Honor—to bounce back from the wounds of war, return to the country of his enemy, and do something to benefit that country—something for the good of all Vietnamese. From his viewpoint as an ambassador living among the North Vietnamese population, abandoning Vietnamese market potential would do more harm than good. In his opinion, the renewal of the Jackson-Vanik waiver "allows America to do what it does best and that is to bring nations into the world community and, at the same time, help those nations learn how to market their product and develop their incredibly efficient human resources. And Vietnam has all of those. Why would we take a walk on that? Why would we not do that? What is the alternative? The alternative is to essentially isolate Vietnam."[7] Peterson saw this engagement as a path to prosperity and, eventually, enlightenment for the whole nation. The waiver was renewed, and Vietnam, like many former and existing communist countries, slowly became more capitalistic and more culturally open—because of the influence of the U.S. dollar.

Much like Peterson, all the former Vietnam POWs continue to live and promulgate the mission Return with Honor. They know their successes can help future POWs, their nation, and future generations. Refusing to rest on their laurels, they continue to give back. With sixteen generals, six admirals, two U.S. ambassadors, two college presidents, one presidential candidate, one vice presidential candidate, two U.S. senators, two U.S. representatives, a state governor, several state legislators, and numerous presidential political appointments in their ranks, it is difficult to overstate their leadership impact on this nation.[8]

If you, like the Hanoi Hilton POWs, want to be part of a culture that outlives you, a culture that carries forward the values and mission your group commonly embraces today, you will have to share the POWs' singularly focused belief that what you are doing has meaning and will continue to have meaning and value.

If you are part of a high-performance team that is continually learning, that is willing to make mistakes in order to succeed, that puts mission ahead of personal interests while protecting individual team members, the chances are high that your culture will remain relevant, no matter what the future holds.

You have read the results of one of the most unusual human performance experiments in history. You read how thr Hanoi Hilton POWs engaged in a balancing act of ideas in tension: self-confidence and humility, self-awareness that recognizes both personal strengths and personal weaknesses, personal ambition balanced by a desire to collaborate on a team effort, brutal honesty about their fears, and confidence in their ability to withstand almost any external challenge they faced without sacrificing their mission. You learned how this group of men successfully created a legacy culture that was marked by all the traits of a high-performance, championship team. That culture endures to this day.

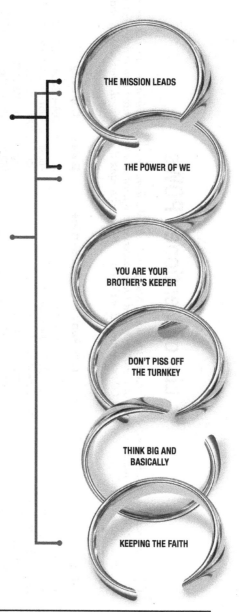

FIGURE 11.1 ~ How High-Performance Teams Are Built

The POWs' culture developed along the "forming-storming-norming-performing" model that is common to high-performance teams. Their culture allowed the "storming" process to be worked through. There were strong disagreements—and many exist to this day. But at the end of the forming and storming processes, individual and collective commitment was to solidarity of purpose and mission.

The Hanoi Hilton POWs' willingness to check their egos at the cell door allowed them to shape many highly competitive, take-charge personalities into a high-performance team. This personal humility was modeled by their leaders and became a trademark of their culture.

THE MISSION LEADS

THE POWER OF WE

YOU ARE YOUR BROTHER'S KEEPER

DON'T PISS OFF THE TURNKEY

THINK BIG AND BASICALLY

KEEPING THE FAITH

APPENDIX

List of Mentioned POWs

A note regarding ranks: Ranks are not used in the book. Many of the POWs were promoted while in captivity, so their ranks changed over time. In addition, many of them continued their careers and retired at a much more senior rank. For reference, this list contains the full names of the POWs mentioned in this book, the highest rank they attained, their service, and the dates of their captivity.

Name	Highest Rank Attained/Service	Dates of Captivity
Everett Alvarez Jr.	Commander, U.S. Navy	August 5, 1964–February 12, 1973
Edwin Lee Atterberry	Captain, U.S. Air Force	August 12, 1967–unknown (died in captivity)
Charles Graham Boyd	General, U.S. Air Force	April 22, 1966–February 12, 1973
Michael Lee Brazelton	Colonel, U.S. Air Force	August 7, 1966–March 4, 1973
Edward Alan Brudno	Captain, U.S. Air Force	October 18, 1965–February 12, 1973
Fred Vann Cherry	Colonel, U.S. Air Force	October 22, 1965–February 12, 1973
Michael Durhan Christian	Lieutenant Commander, U.S. Navy	April 24, 1967–March 4, 1973
George Thomas Coker	Commander, U.S. Navy	August 27, 1966–March 4, 1973
George Everette "Bud" Day	Colonel, U.S. Air Force	August 26, 1967–March 14, 1973
Jeremiah Andrew Denton Jr.	Rear Admiral, U.S. Navy	July 19, 1966–February 12, 1973
John Arthur Dramesi	Colonel, U.S. Air Force	April 2, 1967–March 4, 1973
Leon "Lee" Francis Ellis	Colonel, U.S. Air Force	November 7, 1967–March 14, 1973
John Peter Flynn	Colonel, U.S. Air Force	October 27, 1967–March 14, 1973
Norman Carl Gaddis	Brigadier General, U.S. Air Force	May 12, 1967–March 4, 1973

Paul Edward Galanti	Commander, U.S. Navy	June 6, 1966–February 12, 1973
Porter Alex Halyburton	Commander, U.S. Navy	October 17, 1965–February 12, 1973
Carlyle Smith "Smitty" Harris	Captain, U.S. Air Force	April 4, 1965–February 12, 1973
Samuel Robert Johnson	Colonel, U.S. Air Force	April 16, 1966–February 12, 1973
Phillip A. Kientzler	Lieutenant Commander, U.S. Navy	January 27, 1973–March 27, 1973
Rodney Allen Knutson	Captain, U.S. Navy	October 17, 1965–February 12, 1973
James Lesley Lamar	Lieutenant Colonel, U.S. Air Force	May 6, 1966–February 12, 1973
Gordon Albert "Swede" Larson	Colonel, U.S. Air Force	March 5, 1967–March 4, 1973
Vernon Peyton Ligon	Colonel, U.S. Air Force	November 19, 1967–March 14, 1973
John Sidney McCain III	Captain, U.S. Navy	October 26, 1967–March 14, 1973
Norman Alexander McDaniel	Colonel, U.S. Air Force	July 20, 1966–February 12, 1973
Edward John Mechenbier	Major General, U.S. Air Force	June 14, 1967–February 18, 1973
James Alfred Mulligan	Captain, U.S. Navy	March 20, 1966–February 12, 1973
Thomas Vance Parrott	Colonel, U.S. Air Force	August 12, 1967–March 14, 1973
Douglas Brian "Pete" Peterson	Colonel, U.S. Air Force	September 10, 1966–March 4, 1973
Robinson "Robbie" Risner	Brigadier General, U.S. Air Force	September 16,1965–February 12, 1973
Howard Elmer Rutledge	Captain, U.S. Navy	November 28, 1965–February 12, 1973
Robert Ralston Sawhill	Colonel, U.S. Air Force	August 23, 1967–March 14, 1973
Jerry Allen Singleton	Lieutenant Colonel, U.S. Air Force	November 6, 1965–February 12, 1973
Hugh Alan "Al" Stafford	Commander, U.S. Navy	August 31, 1967–March 14, 1973
James Bond Stockdale	Vice Admiral, U.S. Navy	September 9, 1965–February 12, 1973
Richard Allen Stratton	Captain, U.S. Navy	January 5, 1967–March 4, 1973
Orson George Swindle	Lieutenant Colonel, U.S. Marine Corps	November 11, 1966–March 4, 1973
Charles Nels Tanner	Lieutenant Commander, U.S. Navy	October 9, 1966–March 4, 1973
Charles Peter Zuhoski	Commander, U.S. Navy	July 31, 1967–March 14, 1973

Book Club Discussion Guide

1. Which POW did you identify with most often? Why?
2. Which POW did you wish you could be more like in his outlook on the adversity he faced? Why?
3. Do you think it takes a special person to survive extreme adversity, or can everyday people learn—or even grow stronger—during a crisis?
4. If you believe people can grow during a life crisis, what are some of the elements that make growth possible?
5. If you believe it takes a special type of person, what characteristics make survival possible under extreme conditions?
6. James Stockdale followed a basic philosophy of the Greek sage Epictetus: *You are responsible for what you do with the challenges life hands you.* Do you agree with that philosophy?
7. If you agree with it, what difficulty has most helped you learn to live it?
8. Where is this philosophy most difficult to apply in your life?
9. A basic underpinning of the POW culture was the drive to communicate with and support each other. Tough fighter pilots became more emotionally mature human beings over time as they communicated with and nurtured each other. What role does open communication play in building personal and group maturity?
10. Sports psychology teaches what the POWs learned: *stop wasting energy on things you cannot control and focus on the one thing you can control—yourself.* Where could that lesson be helpful in your professional or personal life?
11. Navy SEALs and the POWs share a common approach to huge—seemingly insurmountable—problems: *Eat the elephant one bite at a time* and accept what has been coined the "Stockdale Paradox" by recognizing the

brutal reality of your current plight but never losing hope that you will eventually prevail. Where could that patient and methodical approach to a big issue help you professionally or personally?

12. What are some of the things that help a person develop that type of patience and persistence?

13. What role does optimism play in this approach? If you were faced with an extreme challenge—one requiring either physical or mental endurance—what tips could you draw from the POWs' or Navy SEALs' experiences to increase your degree of optimism?

14. One military psychiatrist noted the POW pilots were different from other military pilots he saw daily: "[H]e immediately noticed less of a swagger and maybe a bit more grace. They seemed more humble and grateful to him." Can adversity make us humbler human beings?

15. What tips the scale between whether adversity breaks us or helps us mature? Do you think that, when subjected to adversity, you could successfully reframe the experience and recognize potential benefits from the experience? Could you be a candidate for Post-Traumatic Growth (PTG)? If so, how?

Notes

PREFACE. THE MAN IN THE CORNER CELL

The quotes by James Stockdale on pages xvii, xviii, and xix were reprinted from *A Vietnam Experience: Ten Years of Reflection,* by James B. Stockdale, with permission of the publisher, Hoover Institution Press. Copyright © 1984 by the Board of Trustees of the Leland Stanford Junior University.

1. *Atlantic Monthly*, April 1978, reprinted in James B. Stockdale, *A Vietnam Experience: Ten Years of Reflection* (Stanford, CA: Hoover Institution, Stanford University, 1984), 27.
2. *New York Times*, April 1, 1973, reprinted in Stockdale, *Vietnam Experience*, 4.
3. Ibid.
4. Epictetus, *The Enchiridion* (New York: ClassicBooks America, 2009).
5. Stockdale, *Vietnam Experience*, 4.
6. Robert E. Hain, Jeffrey L. Moore, Steve Linnville, and Francine Segovia, interview by the authors, August 23, 2010.
7. Epictetus, *Enchiridion*.
8. James B. Stockdale and Sybil Stockdale, *In Love and War: The Story of a Family's Ordeal and Sacrifice during the Vietnam Years* (New York: Harper & Row, 1984), 156.

INTRODUCTION

1. The description of Dr. William H. Sledge's meetings with returning POWs from the Hanoi Hilton is based on the authors' phone interview with the doctor on April 12, 2012.
2. William H. Sledge, James A. Boydstun, and Alton J. Rabe, "Self-Concept Changes Related to War Captivity," *Archives of General Psychiatry* 37, no. 4 (April 1980): 431.

3. Ibid., 443.
4. Ibid.

CHAPTER 1. THE ROSETTA STONE

1. Nathaniel Zinsser, interview by the authors, November 15, 2010; and Zinsser, phone interview by the authors, November 18, 2011.
2. Ibid.
3. Ibid.
4. Ibid.
5. Charles G. Boyd, interview by the authors, May 3, 2011.
6. Ibid.

CHAPTER 2. LUCKY OR LEARNED

1. Jamie Howren and Taylor Baldwin Kiland, *Open Doors: Vietnam POWs Thirty Years Later* (Washington, DC: Potomac Books, 2005), 4.
2. J. L. Moore, J. Monestersky, C. Ciccone, and M. R. Ambrose, *The Five As of Aviator Personality* (Pensacola, FL: Mitchell Center for POW Studies and Naval Aerospace Medical Institute, 1993).
3. Jeffrey Moore, phone interview by the authors, July 6, 2011.
4. Ibid.
5. Catherine L. Cohan, Steven Cole, and Joanne Davila, *Risk and Resilience Following Repatriation: Marital Transitions Among Vietnam-Era Repatriated Prisoners of War* (State College: Pennsylvania University Population Research Institute, December 2003), 5.
6. George A. Bonanno, interview by the authors, November 15, 2010.
7. Everett Alvarez Jr. and Anthony S. Pitch, *Chained Eagle* (New York: Dell Publishing, 1989), 93.
8. Howren and Kiland, *Open Doors*, 4.
9. Alvarez and Pitch, *Chained Eagle*, 93.
10. Albert Ellis and Windy Dryden, *The Practice of Rational Emotive Behavior Therapy*, 2nd ed. (New York: Springer, 1997), 2.
11. Eric G. Potterat, interview by the authors, August 19, 2010.

12. Ellis and Dryden, *Practice of Rational Emotive Behavior Therapy,* 21.

13. Paul T. Bartone, "Resilience under Military Operational Stress: Can Leaders Influence Hardiness?" *Military Psychology* 18 (2006): S137.

CHAPTER 3. THE MISSION LEADS

The quote by James Stockdale on page 34 reprinted from *A Vietnam Experience: Ten Years of Reflection,* by James B. Stockdale, with permission of the publisher, Hoover Institution Press. Copyright © 1984 by the Board of Trustees of the Leland Stanford Junior University.

1. Sam Johnson and Jan Winebrenner, *Captive Warriors: A Vietnam POW's Story* (College Station: Texas A&M University Press, 1992), 45–46.

2. Kathleen Black, e-mail to the authors, August 4, 2011.

3. Ibid.

4. Ibid.

5. Victor E. Frankl, *Man's Search for Meaning* (Boston: Beacon Press, 2006), 67.

6. Ibid., 70–72.

7. Ibid., 110–11.

8. Ibid.

9. Stuart I. Rochester and Frederick T. Kiley, *Honor Bound: American Prisoners of War in Southeast Asia, 1961– 1973* (Annapolis, MD: U.S. Naval Institute Press, 1999), 129.

10. James Stockdale, "Experiences as a POW in Vietnam" (address to Executives' Club of Chicago), *Naval War College Review*, January–February 1974, reprinted in *A Vietnam Experience*, 7.

11. Frieda Lee Mock and Terry Sanders, *Return with Honor: The American Experience* (Washington, DC: PBS, 1999).

12. Nam-POWs, "Three's In—The Vietnam POW Home Page," June 8, 2002, http://www.nampows.org.

CHAPTER 4. YOU ARE YOUR BROTHER'S KEEPER

The quotes by James Stockdale on pages 40 and 43 were reprinted from *Thoughts of a Philosophical Fighter Pilot,* by James B. Stockdale, with permission of the publisher,

Hoover Institution Press. Copyright © 1995 by the Board of Trustees of the Leland Stanford Junior University.

1. James Bond Stockdale, "Our Personal and National Resolve" (speech to the American Society of Naval Engineers, April 8, 1987), in *Thoughts of a Philosophical Fighter Pilot* (Stanford, CA: Hoover Institution Press, 1995), 49.
2. Johnson and Winebrenner, *Captive Warriors,* 122–23
3. James S. Hirsch, *Two Souls Indivisible: The Friendship That Saved Two POWs in Vietnam* (Boston: Houghton Mifflin, 2005), 73.
4. Ibid., 74.
5. Ibid., 106.
6. Ibid., 142.
7. Stockdale, *Thoughts of a Philosophical Fighter Pilot,* 6.
8. Robert K. Greenleaf, *Servant Leadership: A Journey into the Nature of Legitimate Power and Greatness,* 25th anniversary ed., ed. Larry C. Spears (New York: Paulist Press, 2002).
9. Lee Ellis, *Leading with Honor: Leadership Lessons from the Hanoi Hilton* (Cumming, GA: FreedomStar Media, 2012), 133.
10. Robinson Risner, *The Passing of the Night: My Seven Years as a Prisoner of the North Vietnamese* (New York: Random House, 1973), 108–9.
11. Stockdale, *Thoughts of a Philosophical Fighter Pilot,* 198.
12. Steven Hobfall et al., "Five Essential Elements of Immediate and Mid-Term Mass Trauma Intervention: Empirical Evidence," *Psychiatry* 70, no. 4 (Winter 2007): 284.

CHAPTER 5. THINK BIG AND BASICALLY

The quotes by James Stockdale on pages 53 and 54 were reprinted from *Thoughts of a Philosophical Fighter Pilot,* by James B. Stockdale, with permission of the publisher, Hoover Institution Press. Copyright © 1995 by the Board of Trustees of the Leland Stanford Junior University.

1. Stockdale, *Thoughts of a Philosophical Fighter Pilot,* 28–29.
2. Ibid., 61.

3. James Bond Stockdale, *Courage under Fire: Testing Epictetus's Doctrines in a Laboratory of Human Behavior* (Stanford, CA: Hoover Institution Press, 1993), as quoted in *Thoughts of a Philosophical Fighter Pilot*, 196.

4. Stockdale, *Thoughts of a Philosophical Fighter Pilot*, 49.

5. Ibid., 65–66.

6. Ibid., 196.

7. Edward John Mechenbier, phone interviews by the authors, August 22, 2011, and February 22, 2012.

CHAPTER 6. NO EXCUSES

The quotes by James Stockdale on pages 61, 64, and 67 were reprinted from *Thoughts of a Philosophical Fighter Pilot,* by James B. Stockdale, with permission of the publisher, Hoover Institution Press. Copyright © 1995 by the Board of Trustees of the Leland Stanford Junior University.

1. Paul Galanti, phone interview by the authors, July 29, 2011.

2. Ibid.

3. Stockdale, *Thoughts of a Philosophical Fighter Pilot*, 199.

4. Ibid., 140.

5. David Benedek, interview by the authors, March 9, 2011.

6. Stockdale, *Thoughts of a Philosophical Fighter Pilot*, 140.

7. Ibid., 241.

8. James Clavell, *King Rat* (New York: Dell Publishing, 1962), 7.

9. Ibid., 17.

10. Ibid., 79.

11. Hamish Ion, "Brass Hats behind Bamboo Palisades: Senior Officer POWs in Singapore, Taiwan, and Manchukuo, 1942–45," *Canadian Journal of History*, Autumn 2011, 309.

12. Stockdale, *Thoughts of a Philosophical Fighter Pilot*, 41.

CHAPTER 7. DON'T PISS OFF THE TURNKEY

The quotes by James Stockdale on pages 69 and 73 were reprinted from *Thoughts of a Philosophical Fighter Pilot,* by James B. Stockdale, with permission of the publisher,

Hoover Institution Press. Copyright © 1995 by the Board of Trustees of the Leland Stanford Junior University.

1. Charlie Zuhoski, interview by the authors, May 3, 2011; and Zuhoski, phone interview by the authors, March 18, 2012.
2. Stockdale, *Thoughts of a Philosophical Fighter Pilot*, 28–29.
3. Sam Johnson, interview by the authors, July 27, 2011.
4. Ibid.
5. Ibid.
6. Ibid.
7. Stockdale, *Thoughts of a Philosophical Fighter Pilot*, 63.
8. Everett Alvarez Jr., *Code of Conduct*, with Samuel Schreiner Jr. (New York: Donald L. Fine, 1991), 205–6.
9. Ibid.
10. James A. Mulligan, *The Hanoi Commitment* (Virginia Beach, VA: RIF Marketing, 1981), 189.
11. Geoffrey Norman, *Bouncing Back: How a Heroic Band of POWs Survived Vietnam* (New York: Pocket Books, 1990), 200–202.
12. Mulligan, *Hanoi Commitment*, 189.
13. Rochester and Kiley, *Honor Bound*, 545.
14. Tony Schwartz, "Manage Your Energy, Not Your Time," *Harvard Business Review*, October 2007, 64.
15. Jim Loehr and Tony Schwartz, *The Power of Full Engagement: Managing Energy, Not Time, Is the Key to High Performance and Personal Renewal* (New York: Free Press, 2003), 5.
16. Zinsser interviews, November 15, 2010, and November 18, 2011.
17. John McCain, speech at the Republican National Convention, New Orleans, LA, August 15, 1988, http://en.wikisource.org/wiki/Remarks_by_John_McCain_at_the_1988_Republican_National_Convention.
18. Ibid.

CHAPTER 8. GET ON THE WALL

The quote by James Stockdale on page 83 was reprinted from *Thoughts of a Philosophical Fighter Pilot*, by James

B. Stockdale, with permission of the publisher, Hoover Institution Press. Copyright © 1995 by the Board of Trustees of the Leland Stanford Junior University.

1. Risner, *Passing of the Night*, 108.
2. Ibid., 28.
3. Norman, *Bouncing Back*, 31.
4. Ibid., 33–34.
5. Ibid., 50–51.
6. Dick Stratton, quoted in Alvarez, *Code of Conduct*, 172.
7. Martha Beck, "Before You Confess Your Deep, Dark Secrets . . . ," *Oprah*, June 2002.
8. Lawrence G. Calhoun and Richard G. Tedeschi, *Handbook of Posttraumatic Growth: Research and Practice* (Mahwah, NJ: Lawrence Erlbaum Associates, 2009), 12.
9. Ibid., 13.
10. Ibid., 33.
11. Richard Tedeschi, interview by the authors, March 8, 2011.
12. Calhoun and Tedeschi, *Handbook of Posttraumatic Growth*, 7.

CHAPTER 9. KEEPING THE FAITH

The quote by James Stockdale on page 103 was reprinted from *Thoughts of a Philosophical Fighter Pilot,* by James B. Stockdale, with permission of the publisher, Hoover Institution Press. Copyright © 1995 by the Board of Trustees of the Leland Stanford Junior University.

1. Steve Combs, phone interview by the authors, March 10, 2012.
2. Galanti interview, July 29, 2011.
3. Ibid.
4. Combs interview.
5. F. Segovia, J. L. Moore, S. E. Linnville, R. Hoyt, and R. E. Hain, "Optimism Predicts Resilience in Repatriated Prisoners of War: A 37-Year Longitudinal Study," *Journal of Traumatic Stress* 25, no. 3 (June 2012): 330–36.
6. Potterat interview.
7. Ibid.

8. Andy Morgan, interview by the authors, November 14, 2010.
9. Potterat interview.
10. Zinsser interview, November 18, 2011.
11. Zuhoski interview, May 3, 2011
12. Zuhoski interview, March 18, 2012.
13. Ibid.
14. Stockdale, *Thoughts of a Philosophical Fighter Pilot*, 51.
15. Ibid., 39.
16. Josh Butner, interview by the authors, August 19, 2010.
17. Potterat interview.

CHAPTER 10. THE POWER OF WE

1. Rochester and Kiley, *Honor Bound*, 530.
2. Risner, *Passing of the Night*, 218.
3. Ibid., 219.
4. Ibid.
5. Ibid., 221.
6. Galanti interview.
7. Mechenbier interview, February 22, 2012.
8. Zinsser interview, November 18, 2011.

CONCLUSION

1. Bruce W. Tuckman, "Developmental Sequence in Small Groups," *Psychological Bulletin* 63, no. 6 (1965): 384–99.
2. Mechenbier interviews, August 22, 2011, and February 22, 2012.
3. Ibid.
4. Pete Peterson, quoted in Sandy Northrop, *Pete Peterson: Assignment Hanoi* (Washington, DC: PBS, 1999).
5. Pete Peterson, quoted in ibid.
6. *Disapproving Waiver of Jackson-Vanik Freedom of Emigration Requirements for Vietnam: Hearing on S. J. Res. 47 before the Subcommittee on International Trade of the Finance Committee*, 105th Cong. (1998) (statement of Senator Bob Smith).
7. Northrop, *Pete Peterson*.
8. Howren and Kiland, *Open Doors*, 157–59.

Selected Bibliography

Alvarez, Everett, Jr. *Code of Conduct*. With Samuel Schreiner Jr. New York: Donald L. Fine, 1991.

Alvarez, Everett, Jr., and Anthony S. Pitch. *Chained Eagle*. New York: Dell Publishing, 1989.

Bartlett, Tom. "Soldiers of Optimism: Is New Army Psychology Program Simply a Shot in the Dark?" *Chronicle of Higher Education*, October 30, 2011.

Bartone, Paul T. "Resilience under Military Operational Stress: Can Leaders Influence Hardiness?" *Military Psychology* 18 (2006): S131–48.

———. "To Build Resilience: Leader Influence on Mental Hardiness." *Defense Horizons*, November 2009, 1–8.

Beck, Martha. "Before You Confess Your Deep, Dark Secrets . . ." *Oprah*, June 2002.

Calhoun, Lawrence G., and Richard G. Tedeschi. *Handbook of Posttraumatic Growth: Research and Practice*. Mahwah, NJ: Lawrence Erlbaum Associates, 2009.

Clavell, James. *King Rat*. New York: Dell Publishing, 1962.

Cohan, Catherine L., Steven Cole, and Joanne Davila. *Risk and Resilience Following Repatriation: Marital Transitions among Vietnam-Era Repatriated Prisoners of War*. State College: Pennsylvania State University Population Research Institute, December 2003.

Cornum, Rhonda, Michael D. Matthews, and Martin E. P. Seligman. "Comprehensive Soldier Fitness: Building Resilience in a Challenging Institutional Context." *American Psychologist* 66, no. 1 (January 2011): 4–9.

Ellis, Albert, and Windy Dryden. *The Practice of Rational Emotive Behavior Therapy*. 2nd ed. New York: Springer, 1997.

Ellis, Lee. *Leading with Honor: Leadership Lessons from the Hanoi Hilton*. Cumming, GA: FreedomStar Media, 2012.

Epictetus. *The Enchiridion.* New York: ClassicBooks
America, 2009.

Frankl, Viktor E. *Man's Search for Meaning.* Boston: Beacon
Press, 2006.

Gifford, Robert K., Robert J. Ursano, John S. Stuart, and
Charles C. Engel. "Stress and Stressors of the Early
Phases of the Persian Gulf War." *Philosophical
Transactions of the Royal Society* 361, no. 1468
(April 2006): 585–91.

Gladwell, Malcolm. "Getting Over It." *New Yorker,*
November 8, 2004, 75–79.

Greenleaf, Robert K. *Servant Leadership: A Journey into the
Nature of Legitimate Power and Greatness.* Edited by
Larry Spears. 25th ed. New York: Paulist Press, 2002.

Guarino, Larry. *A POW's Story: 2801 Days in Hanoi.* New
York: Ivy Books, 1990.

Henman, Linda D. "The Vietnam Prisoner of War
Experience: Links between Communication and
Resilience." PhD diss., Fielding Institute, 1998.

Hirsch, James S. *Two Souls Indivisible: The Friendship That
Saved Two POWs in Vietnam.* Boston: Houghton
Mifflin, 2005.

Hobfall, Steven, et al. "Five Essential Elements of Immediate
and Mid-Term Mass Trauma Intervention: Empirical
Evidence." *Psychiatry* 70, no. 4 (Winter 2007):
283–315.

Howes, Craig. *Voices of the Vietnam POWs: Witnesses to
Their Fight.* New York: Oxford University Press, 1993.

Howren, Jamie, and Taylor Baldwin Kiland. *Open Doors:
Vietnam POWs Thirty Years Later.* Washington, DC:
Potomac Books, 2005.

Ion, Hamish. "Brass Hats behind Bamboo Palisades:
Senior Officer POWs in Singapore, Taiwan, and
Manchukuo, 1942–45." *Canadian Journal of
History,* Autumn 2011, 304–31.

Johnson, Sam, and Jan Winebrenner. *Captive Warriors: A
Vietnam POW's Story.* College Station: Texas A&M
University Press, 1992.

Lawrence, William P., and Rosario Rausa. *Tennessee Patriot:
The Naval Career of Vice Admiral William P.*

Lawrence. Annapolis, MD: Naval Institute Press, 2006.

Loehr, Jim, and Tony Schwartz. *The Power of Full Engagement: Managing Energy, Not Time, Is the Key to High Performance and Personal Renewal*. New York: Free Press, 2003.

Mock, Freida Lee, and Terry Sanders. *Return with Honor: The American Experience*. Washington, DC: PBS, 1999.

Moore, J. L., J. Monestersky, C. Ciccone, and M. R. Ambrose. *The Five As of Aviator Personality*. Pensacola, FL: Mitchell Center for POW Studies and Naval Aerospace Medical Institute, 1993.

Mulligan, James A. *The Hanoi Commitment*. Virginia Beach, VA: RIF Marketing, 1981.

Nam-POWs. "Three's In—The Vietnam POW Home Page." June 8, 2002. http://www.nampows.org.

Norman, Geoffrey. *Bouncing Back: How a Heroic Band of POWs Survived Vietnam*. New York: Pocket Books, 1990.

Northrop, Sandy. *Pete Peterson: Assignment Hanoi*. Washington, DC: PBS, 1999.

Reich, John W., Alex J. Zautra, and John Stuart Hall, eds. *Handbook of Adult Resilience*. New York: Guilford Press, 2010.

Risner, Robinson. *The Passing of the Night: My Seven Years as a Prisoner of the North Vietnamese*. New York: Random House, 1973.

Rochester, Stuart I., and Frederick T. Kiley. *Honor Bound: American Prisoners of War in Southeast Asia, 1961– 1973*. Annapolis, MD: U.S. Naval Institute Press, 1999.

Schwartz, Tony. "Manage Your Energy, Not Your Time." *Harvard Business Review*, October 2007. http://hbr. org/2007/10/manage-your-energy-not-your-time/ar/1.

Segovia, F., J. L. Moore, S. E. Linnville, R. Hoyt, and R. E. Hain. "Optimism Predicts Resilience in Repatriated Prisoners of War: A 37-Year Longitudinal Study." *Journal of Traumatic Stress* 25, no. 3 (June 2012): 330–36.

Sherman, Nancy. "A Crack in the Stoic's Armor." *New York Times*, May 30, 2010.

Sherwood, Ben. *The Survivors Club: The Secrets and Science That Could Save Your Life*. New York: Grand Central Publishing, 2009.

Sledge, William H., James A. Boydstun, and Alton J. Rabe. "Self-Concept Changes Related to War Captivity." *Archives of General Psychiatry* 37, no. 4 (April 1980): 430–43

Stix, Gary. "The Neuroscience of True Grit." *Scientific American*, March 2011, 28–33.

Stockdale, James Bond. *Courage under Fire: Testing Epictetus's Doctrines in a Laboratory of Human Behavior*. Stanford, CA: Hoover Institution Press, 1993.

———. *Thoughts of a Philosophical Fighter Pilot*. Stanford, CA: Hoover Institution Press, 1995.

———. *A Vietnam Experience: Ten Years of Reflection* Stanford, CA: Hoover Institution Press, 1984.

Stockdale, James B., and Sybil Stockdale. *In Love and War: The Story of a Family's Ordeal and Sacrifice During the Vietnam Years*. New York: Harper & Row, 1984.

Swindle, Orson. "Always Leading and Always Will." *Proceedings*, August 2005, 64.

Tuckman, Bruce W. "Developmental Sequence in Small Groups." *Psychological Bulletin* 63, no. 6 (1965): 384–99.

Index

Page numbers followed by an *f* indicate figures.

About the Authors

Raised in a military family, TAYLOR BALDWIN KILAND was seven years old and living in Coronado, California, when she witnessed the POWs' homecoming. This event sparked her lifelong interest in them. In 2000 and 2008 she volunteered for Senator John McCain's presidential campaigns, during which she met many of the former POWs. She is the author or coauthor of three other books, including *Open Doors: Vietnam POWs Thirty Years Later*, a close look at the current lives of thirty former Vietnam POWs. A former Naval officer, Taylor is now a management consultant with a large technology and strategy consulting firm and lives in Alexandria, Virginia.

PETER FRETWELL's interest in the Hanoi Hilton leadership and organizational culture began during his MBA studies in strategic leadership. The writings of James Stockdale convinced him that the lessons the POWs brought home could benefit other organizations. *Lessons from the Hanoi Hilton* is the result of more than seven years of research and study on the topic.

The **Naval Institute Press** is the book-publishing arm of the U.S. Naval Institute, a private, nonprofit, membership society for sea service professionals and others who share an interest in naval and maritime affairs. Established in 1873 at the U.S. Naval Academy in Annapolis, Maryland, where its offices remain today, the Naval Institute has members worldwide.

Members of the Naval Institute support the education programs of the society and receive the influential monthly magazine *Proceedings* or the colorful bimonthly magazine *Naval History* and discounts on fine nautical prints and on ship and aircraft photos. They also have access to the transcripts of the Institute's Oral History Program and get discounted admission to any of the Institute-sponsored seminars offered around the country.

The Naval Institute's book-publishing program, begun in 1898 with basic guides to naval practices, has broadened its scope to include books of more general interest. Now the Naval Institute Press publishes about seventy titles each year, ranging from how-to books on boating and navigation to battle histories, biographies, ship and aircraft guides, and novels. Institute members receive significant discounts on the Press's more than eight hundred books in print.

Full-time students are eligible for special half-price membership rates. Life memberships are also available.

For a free catalog describing Naval Institute Press books currently available, and for further information about joining the U.S. Naval Institute, please write to:

Member Services
U.S. Naval Institute
291 Wood Road
Annapolis, MD 21402-5034
Telephone: (800) 233-8764
Fax: (410) 571-1703
Web address: www.usni.org